Python Programming For Beginners In 2021

Learn Python

In 5 Days With Step-by-Step

Guidance, **Hands-On Exercises**

And **Solution**

[Fun Tutorial For Novice Programmers]

By

James Tudor

www.MillenniumPublishingLimited.com

www.MillenniumPublishingLimited.com

Copyright ©2021

All rights reserved. Except as permitted under the U.S. Copyright Act of 1976, the scanning, uploading and distribution of this book via the Internet or via any other means without the express permission of the author is illegal and punishable by law. Please purchase only authorized electronic editions, and do not participate in or encourage electronic piracy of copyrighted material.

Table of Contents

Who Is This Book For? 5

What Is Python? 6
   Interpreted Not Compiled 6
   Advantages of Python as an Interpreted Language 6
   Scripts 7
   Python as a General Purpose Programming Language ... 7
   Community Frameworks, Toolkits, Libraries, and Modules ... 7
   Programming Paradigms and Object Oriented Programming ... 8
   History, Background, and Evolution 8
   Core Philosophy and Uniqueness 9
   Summary 9

Chapter 1 11
Getting Started With Python 11
   Python 2.x vs. Python 3.x 11
   Installing the Interpreter 11
   Using Python Shell and IDLE 12
   Writing Your First Program 12
   Shell, IDLE, and Scripts Syntax 13
   Prompt 13
   Indentation 13
   Indentation Prompt 14
   Python Shell Navigation 15
   IDLE Navigation 15
   Troubleshooting Installation Issues 15
   Practice Exercise 16
   Chapter Summary 16

Chapter 2 18
Variables and Operators 18
   Computer Basics 18
   Computer Program 19
   What Are Variables? 19
   Naming Variables 21
   Using Variables 22
   Naming Conventions 22
   Naming by Description 22
   Introduction to Expressions and Python Operators 25
   Expressions 25
   Operators 25
   Arithmetic Operators 26
   Relational Operators 26
   Assignment Operator 27
   Logical Operators 28
   Truth Table 29
   Membership Operators 29
   Identity Operators 30

   Bitwise Operators 31
   Practice Exercise 32
   Chapter Summary 33

Chapter 2: Solution 34

Chapter 3 37
Simple Data Types 37
   Numbers 37
   String 38
   Combining/Concatenating strings 38
   Avoiding Type Errors with Conversion Functions 38
   Avoiding, Replacing, and Stripping Whitespace 40
   Avoiding syntax errors with strings 42
   Collections/Sequences 43
   Tuple 53
   Dictionary 56
   Styling your code 60
   General Style Guide 61
   Indentation 61
   Line length 61
   Blank lines 62
   Practice Exercise 62
   Chapter Summary 63

Chapter 3: Solution 64

Chapter 4 66
Conditions and Loops 66
   "if" statements 67
   Else Statements 67
   Code Blocks 68
   Loops 68
   While 68
   For Loop 69
   Break 69
   Continue 71
   Error Handling 72
   Try and Except 72
   Variable Styling 73
   Practice Exercise 74
   Chapter Summary 77

Chapter 4: Solution 78

Chapter 5 82
Functions and Modules 82
   Arguments and Parameters 82
   Parameters Require Arguments 83
   Multiple Parameters 84

- Passing Arguments By Value, Reference, and Assignment...84
- Returning Value ...87
- Mutable and Immutable Objects...88
- Passing List by Value...90
- Anonymous Functions or Lambda ...91
- Variable Scopes ...91
- Optional Arguments and Default Values ...91
- Arbitrary Arguments...92
- Storing Functions in Modules ...93
- Function and Module Styles ...95
- Practice Exercises ...95
- Chapter Summary...96

Chapter 5: Solution ...97

Chapter 6 ...99
Object Oriented Programming (OOP) ...99
- What is Object Oriented Programming? ...99
- Imperative ...99
- Structured ...99
- Procedural ...99
- Object Oriented ...99
- Creating and Using a Class...100
- Working With Classes and Instances ...101
- Writing Parent and Child Classes ...102
- Default Attribute Value ...103
- Modifying Attribute Values ...103
- Inheritance ...103
- Defining Attributes and Methods for the Child Class ...104
- Using Pass ...105
- The init() Method For Child Class ...106
- Overriding methods from the parent class ...107
- Importing Classes ...109
- Name Mangling ...111
- What is self ...112
- Class and Static Methods...114
- Styling classes ...115
- Practice Exercise ...115
- Chapter Summary...116

Chapter 6: Solution...117

Chapter 7...119
Working With Files ...119
- Reading from a File ...120
- File Pointer ...120
- File Access Modes ...122
- Writing to a File ...123
- Practice Exercise ...123
- Chapter Summary...124

Chapter 7: Solution...125

Chapter 8...127
Exception Handling...127
- What Is Exception Handling...127
- Handling the Zero Division Error Exception...127
- Using Try-Except Blocks ...128
- Reading an Exception Error Trace Back ...130
- Using exceptions to prevent crashes ...130
- The Else Block ...131
- Failing Silently ...133
- Handling the File Not Found Exception Error ...133
- Checking If File Exists ...134
- Try and Except ...134
- Creating a New File ...135
- Practice Exercise ...135
- Chapter Summary...135

Chapter 8: Solution...136

Chapter 9...138
Testing Your Code...138
- Testing a function ...138
- Testing a Class ...141
- Practice Exercise ...141
- Chapter Summary...141

Chapter 9: Solution ...143

What Comes after This?...144

The End ...145

Who Is This Book For?

This book is primarily for people who are relatively new to programming and, more specifically, those who want to discover the world of Python. This book will take you through the fundamentals of programming and Python.

In the first half of this book, you'll discover the basics of programming and common computer data processing. The lessons will familiarize you with how programs work and their primary components.

The second half of this book will equip you with mid-level programming knowledge. There, you'll discover how to code some advanced functionalities and, more importantly, how you can write simple, efficient and readable code.

If you diligently work through the chapter examples and exercises (along with the downloadable solution booklet we've provided), we are confident you'll have a good *fundamental* understanding of python by day 5.

Excited yet? Let's get right to it!

What Is Python?

Put simply, Python is an interpreted, high level programming language for general-purpose programming. Created by Guido van Rossum, Python has a design philosophy that emphasizes code readability, which reduces the cost of program maintenance. It does not require compilation and, much like Java, it is object oriented.

Python's high-level built in data structures, combined with dynamic typing and binding, make it very attractive for Rapid Application Development. It supports multiple programming paradigms, including object oriented, imperative, functional and procedural, and has a large comprehensive library.

The book will explain more about these characteristics later.

Interpreted Not Compiled

A program is a set of instructions that direct a computer's hardware to perform certain tasks. The computer load the instructions in its memory, read the instructions, and execute them one by one.

Creating a program requires a developer to write code using a programming language. Written code alone is not enough to make a program operational since the computer does not understand code written using a programming language.

There are two common ways to make written code an operational program. The first method is **compiling** and the second method is **interpreting**.

Usually, a developer compiles his written code using a compiler. The compiler check the validity of the code and then it translates it to native code or instructions computers can understand. Programming codes of some programming languages like C and C++ require compiling.

However, programs written using Python does not require compiling – instead, they are **interpreted**. A separate program, called the interpreter, runs when a user executes Python code. The interpreter interprets or translates Python code to byte code once a user executes it, which then allows the computer to understand the instructions in the code.

Advantages of Python as an Interpreted Language

The problem with compiled programs in native code is that it only works on the target platform. For example, a program compiled for Windows operating systems will not work in MacOS or UNIX based program. Of course, the user can use a third party program like virtual machines to run the compiled application.

With Python as an interpreted language, a Python developer does not need to worry about that. Since the Python interpreter is basically a virtual machine of sorts, you can run Python code in almost every platform and device available (a very powerful benefit).

Another problem with compiled language is the compilation process itself. Compilation takes time. A small program with a thousand lines of code can take a minute or two to compile.

That seems a small issue at first. However, if you need to debug (i.e. troubleshoot) or perform a test run of your program, you will always need to compile it. And those one to two minutes compile time can easily add up.

Another issue is that you cannot edit the program easily. You always have to edit the source code, recompile, and debug.

An interpreted language like Python does not have those issues. Once you are done with the code, you can just run it. If you are not satisfied, you can just go back on editing your code and run it again. This is why developers like to rely on Python for rapid application development or RAD.

Scripts

Programs written in Python are often referred to as scripts, especially if they are small in size. Scripts are small programs that are executed within a runtime environment. In Python's case, the runtime environment is the Python interpreter.

Most scripts usually deal with text processing. In web development, Python is used as a server-side scripting language. Server-side scripting is basically a technique used in web development which involves employing scripts on a web server which produce a response customized for each user's request to the website. The alternative is for the web server itself to deliver a static web page.

Web developers often use Python as a replacement for other popular server side scripting languages like PHP and ASP.

Python as a General Purpose Programming Language

Python is versatile as mentioned before. People in different industries and field of studies use it. You can use it to create programs with a graphical user interface (GUI). Furthermore, you can develop web servers or cloud applications using Python. Last, but definitely not the least, you can use it to process big data.

Community Frameworks, Toolkits, Libraries, and Modules

Python by itself is a small tool that you can use to develop simple programs and scripts. Because of that, you need to write a lot of code to develop large and complex programs.

However, writing every line of code is tedious and unnecessary for you to achieve or create complex programs. You can always opt for a far easier and practical route: using frameworks and importing libraries and modules.

Frameworks, toolkits, libraries, and modules are files containing written code that you can use to add more functionality to Python and your programs.

For example, creating a simple graphical user interface window in Python is not possible if you do not use frameworks, libraries, modules, or toolkits. Using a toolkit like TkInter will allow you to easily create a GUI.

Thankfully, Python is backed by its huge community. Its community has lots of frameworks, toolkits, libraries, and modules to offer. Most of them are free for you to use. And they can help you immensely in creating robust and complex programs you have in mind.

Programming Paradigms and Object Oriented Programming

Python is an object oriented programming language. Object-oriented programming (OOP) refers to a type of computer programming in which programmers define not only the data type of a data structure, but also the types of operations (functions) that can be applied to the data structure.

In this way, the data structure becomes an object that includes both data and functions. In addition, programmers can create relationships between one object and another e.g. objects can inherit characteristics from other objects.

Furthermore, OOP is a programming paradigm and multiple paradigms have been developed over the years.

A programming paradigm is essentially a methodology on how to write programs. You should bare in mind that writing a program is a constant process of solving problems. With each line of code, you solve a problem that often presents itself as, "How can I write this program to make sure that it will work as I intended to?"

As with any problem, especially those that are mathematical in nature, there are multiple ways to write and solve them. For example, you can write and solve the problem 1 + 1 + 1 as 1 + (1 + 1) or 1 * 3. Despite obvious differences in the way the problem is presented, you still arrive at the same solution, which is 3.

Programming paradigms are like that. They are like disciplines, if you will. Each paradigm has its own advantages and disadvantages. Nonetheless, all of them will allow you to still create a program that will work as you intended.

Python is well suited to object oriented programming. It does not mean that you cannot use other programming paradigms with it. It just means that it is easier to write object oriented programs with it.

We will discuss more about programing paradigms and object oriented programming in later parts of this book.

History, Background, and Evolution

The development of Python started in the 1980s. Guido van Rossum started its implementation in 1989. Rossum decided to name the programming language after Monty Python, a UK based comedy group.

Rossum released Python 2.0 in the year 2000. At the same time, he made the development process transparent and allowed community involvement. He then released Python 3.0 in 2008. This version of Python had major changes, which did not have backwards compatibility (i.e. did not work well) with programs written in previous Python releases.

Due to the limitation of Python 3.0 in terms of compatibility with old source codes, most businesses and developers stuck with Python 2.x. Be that as it may, Python 3.x is equipped with a Python 2.x code conversion tool that makes transition to the latest releases possible. However, some deemed it easier to keep and maintained their old code.

Core Philosophy and Uniqueness

The core philosophies of Python can be summed up to simplicity, transparency, and readability. Rossum and the community behind Python made sure that all programs written in Python can be understood by everyone after reading the code once.

Below are some of the ways Python programming differs from some of the most common programming language conventions:

- You can create code blocks through indentation alone instead of enclosing with brackets to create blocks of code.

- You can end a statement without placing a semicolon (;) or any symbol.

- You can splice in other programs with Python seamlessly and you can use it for different purposes.

- You can create programs with shorter code.

- You do not need to declare variables and define their types.

Summary

Veteran programmers and developers see Python as a versatile and handy tool. They can use it anywhere and anytime they want. It is compatible with multiple platforms.

Inexperienced programmers and total beginners should know that Python is an excellent language to learn. It is a practical choice.

As of now, Python is one of the top 10 most used and popular programming languages in the world. Its usefulness is vast and it continues to grow in popularity. With all of the characteristics it has, it has clear advantages over other programming languages.

Did you know?

There is a poem written by Tim Peters named as The Zen Of Python which can be read by just writing *import this* in the interpreter!

Chapter 1

Getting Started With Python

You can run and code Python on Windows, Mac, and Linux. To get started, head over to the official website: www.python.org and download the Python installer. This book will use Windows as the primary environment for the examples and lessons.

Python 2.x vs. Python 3.x

There are two popular and official versions of Python: Python 3.x and 2.x. As of this writing, you can download Python 3.7.0 if you want the 3.x version. You can also download Python 2.7.15 if you want the 2.x version.

However, to prevent any conflicts and misunderstandings, please download and use Python 3.x. All the examples and lessons in this book are written with Python 3.x in mind.

The 2.x version is an older version of Python. Ever since the Python developers proceeded in developing Python 3.x, they have made a lot of changes to the behavior and even the syntax of the Python programming languages.

For example, if you divide 3 and 2 using the '/' operator in Python 2.x, you will receive an output of 1. If you divide the same numbers with the same operator in Python 3.x, you will receive an output of 1.5.

You may ask: If Python 3.x is new and improved, why are the developers keeping the old versions and why is Python 2.x being used?

The quick answer to that is **code migration**. Because there are many differences between version 2.x and version 3.x, programs and scripts created using version 2.x need to be recoded to become compatible with version 3.x Python.

If you are dealing with a small program using version 2.x, then the code migration will be a trivial problem at best. However, if you have programs with thousands of lines, then migration can become a huge problem. Other issues with migrating to Python 3.x are code maintenance and retraining programmers to adapt with the changes.

Because of the aforementioned reasons, developers with huge programs written and ran using the version 2.x runtime environment did not bother making the transition to version 3.x.

Installing the Interpreter

Python comes with two important 'programs': Python's runtime environment and command line interpreter. The Python installer you download from its website contains both. Installing them is easy, particularly in Windows.

All you need to do is download the file and click open to let it run the setup. You will need to follow a few simple step-by-step instructions, click a few buttons here and there and Python will be available on your computer.

Note that there will be a point during the installation that you will need to select the packages and features that you want to be installed in your system. Make sure that you check all of them.

Note that tcl/tk installs TkInter, which is a Graphic User Interface (GUI) toolkit you need if you plan to create windows for your programs. The Integrated Development and Learning Environment (IDLE) require and depend on TkInter since it is a Python program with a GUI.

Also, for now, check the Python test suite feature. You will need it later. Finally, PIP is an optional feature that allows you to download Python packages later.

If you believe you do not need some of them, just make sure that the checkbox for IDLE and Python Test Suite are selected.

Using Python Shell and IDLE

There are two ways to run a Python program. And that is using its runtime environment or using the command line interpreter. The command line interpreter has two forms. The first one is the regular Python shell. The second one is IDLE or Integrated Development and Learning Environment.

The regular Python shell uses the familiar command line interface (CLI) or terminal look while IDLE is a Python program encased in a regular graphical user interface (GUI) window. IDLE is full of easy to access menu, customization options, and GUI functions while the Python shell is devoid of those and only offer a command prompt (i.e. the input field in a text-based user interface screen).

One of the beneficial functions of IDLE is its syntax highlighting. The syntax highlighting function makes it easier for programmers or scripters to identify between keywords, operators, variables, and numeric literals.

Also, you can customize the highlight color and the font properties displayed on IDLE. With the shell, you only get a monospaced font, white font color, and black background.

All of the examples in this book are written in the Python shell. However, it is okay for you to write using IDLE. It is suited for beginners since they do not need to worry about indentation and code management. Not to mention that the syntax highlighting is truly beneficial.

Writing Your First Program

To get you started, code the below **Hello World** program. It has been a tradition for new programmers to start their learning with this simple program. Just write this line in the shell or IDLE and press Enter.

```
>>> print("Hello World!")
Hello World!
```

Shell, IDLE, and Scripts Syntax

Programming languages, just like a regular human language like English, have grammar/writing rules or syntax. Syntax rules in programming languages are simple but strict.

Unlike humans, the computer and computer programs like compilers and interpreters cannot understand context. They require precise and proper statements to know what you want. A simple syntax error can stop your program from functioning or make the computer terminate your program.

This book will not discuss every syntax rules in this section. It will, instead, teach you one on a need-to-know basis. Syntax rules, after all, are dependent on the things you are writing. And since you do not actually have anything to write yet, this section will introduce you to the basic ones first.

Prompt

The Python Shell and IDLE has a prompt, which looks like this: >>>. You generally start writing your code after the prompt in the Python Shell and IDLE. However, remember that when you write code in a file, py script, or module, you do not need to write the prompt.

For example:

```
class thisClass():

    def function1():

        x = 1

        print(x)


    def function2():

        pass
```

That is valid code.

Indentation

When programming, you will encounter or create code blocks. A *code block* is a piece of Python program text (or statement) that can be executed as a unit, such as a module, a class definition or a function body. They often end with a colon (:).

Some code blocks (like modules) are normally executed only once, others (like function bodies) may be executed many times. Any statement that will be grouped inside the code block must be indented.

By default and by practice, indentation is done with four spaces. You can do away with any number of spaces as long as the code block has a uniform number of spaces before each statement. For example:

```
def function1():
    x = 1
    print(x)

def function2():
        y = "Sample Text"
        print("Nothing to see here.")
```

That is perfectly valid code. You can also use tab, but it is not recommended since it can be confusing and you will get an error if you mix using tabs and spaces. Also, if you change the **number of spaces** for every line of code, you will get an error. Here is an example in the shell. Note the large space before print(x) on line 2.

```
>>> x = 1
>>>     print(x)
  File "<stdin>", line 1
    print(x)
    ^
IndentationError: unexpected indent
>>> _
```

By the way, a statement is a line of code or instruction.

Indentation Prompt

When using the Python Shell, it will tell you when to indent by using the prompt (...). For example:

```
>>> def function1():
    x = 1
    print(x)

>>> def function2():
    y = "Sample Text"
    print("Nothing to see here.")

>>> _
```

In IDLE, indentation will be *automatic*. And to escape an indentation or code block, you can just press Enter or go to the next line.

Python Shell Navigation

You cannot interact using a mouse with the Python Shell. Your mouse will be limited to the window's context menu, window commands such as minimize, maximize, and close, and scrolling.

Also, you can perform marking (selecting), copying, and pasting, but you need to use the windows context menu for that using the mouse. You can also change the appearance of the window and shell by going through the properties menu.

Most of the navigation you can do in the shell is moving the navigation caret (the blinking white underscore). You can move it using the navigation keys (left and right arrow keys, PgUp, PgDn, Home, End, etcetera). The up and down arrow keys' function is to browse through the previous lines you have written.

IDLE Navigation

The IDLE window is just like a regular GUI window. It contains a menu bar where you can access most of IDLE's functionalities. Also, you can use the mouse directly on IDLE's work area as if you are using a regular word processor.

You might need to take a quick look at the menu bar's function for you to familiarize yourself with them. Unlike the Python shell, IDLE provides a lot more helpful features that can help you with programming.

Primarily, IDLE is the main tool you can use to develop Python programs. However, you are not limited to it. You can use other development environment or word processors to create your scripts.

Troubleshooting Installation Issues

First of all, make sure that you download the installation file from the website: https://www.python.org. Next, make sure that you chose the proper installation file for your operating system. There are dedicated installation files for Windows, MacOSX, and other UNIX based operating system.

If your computer is running on Windows XP, the latest release of Python will not work on it. You must install and use Python 3.4. Also, remember that there are two versions of each release: a 32-bit and a 64-bit version. If you are unsure if your computer is running on 32 or 64-bit, then just get the 32-bit version. Normally, the recommended installer that the site will provide contains both and will automatically detect which installer it will use.

Normally, you do not need to go to Python's website to download the installation file if you are using a Linux distribution as an operating system. You can just use your system's package manager.

Before installing Python, **make sure that you have at least 100 MB free disk space**. You can also edit the installation location of Python. However, take note of the location you specify if you wish to install Python in a different folder.

If the installer did not provide shortcuts for you, you can just create them. The Python shell is located in the root folder of your Python installation.

<Python installation folder>\python.exe
For example:

"C:\Python37\python.exe"
For IDLE, you can use its batch file located in

<Python installation folder>\Lib\idlelib\idle.bat
For example:

"C:\Python37\Lib\idlelib\idle.bat"
If you cannot find the idlelib folder inside the Python Lib folder, reinstall Python and make sure that IDLE is checked.

Practice Exercise

For now, familiarize yourself with the Python shell and IDLE. Try to discover the things you can do with them. Look at all the messages that it may send you as you enter information on it.

When it comes to IDLE, try to customize it (e.g. change the color theme from the default IDLE Classic to IDLE Dark). Explore all the other features and functions you can change. Have fun!

Chapter Summary

At this point, you are already a few steps away from writing code and creating programs. Remember that you need Python 3.x while learning the contents of this book. You also need to make sure that you have IDLE and the test suite.

With regards to the coding environment, you have two options: use the shell or IDLE. It is recommended that you use the latter. But if you want to do this intimately and be challenged a bit, you can choose the shell.

Did you know?

In 2009, Swedish programmer Markus "Notch" Persson released the first version of Minecraft, a building game he'd made. By 2014, Minecraft had around 100 million registered users and was sold to Microsoft for $2.5 billion.

Chapter 2

Variables and Operators

Before you learn about operators and variables, you need to have a brief understanding of how a computer functions and what a computer program is.

Computer Basics

A computer's primary function is to compute. It needs data to compute or process. The computer retrieves data from user input, programs, and other input sources like microphones, scanners, computer networks and even the Internet.

A computer has four important components: the central processing unit (CPU), random-access memory (RAM), motherboard (MB), and a power supply unit (PSU). The RAM *temporarily* stores the data the CPU needs to process. The motherboard, which is basically a huge and complex circuit board, houses the CPU and RAM. The power supply, which also connects to the motherboard, supplies power to everything.

A computer can operate or boot (i.e. start up) with those four components alone. The absence of at least one of those components will render the computer unable to boot. Some older computers that do not have built-in graphics processors will require a graphics card to operate.

Other components like keyboards, hard disks, monitors, and graphics cards are additional peripherals you can install to extend the functionality of a computer.

The motherboard also houses the basic input output system (BIOS) chip, which stores a program that allows a computer to operate with only the most basic functionalities.

The BIOS allows the computer to accept basic input and provide basic output. Some basic input processes are accepting keyboard strokes and mouse clicks and movements. Some basic output processes are text and image monitor display and beep sounds.

Aside from handling input and output, the BIOS *finds* and initializes all hardware in the motherboard. It detects and initializes graphics/video cards, sound cards, ethernet adapters, keyboards, mice, mass storage medias (USB drives, hard disk drives (HDD), solid state drives (SSD), etc.), and other built-in functionalities of the mother board.

The BIOS allows the user to perform customization of the motherboard and basic hardware settings. It also allows the booting process of an operating system from a mass storage device or network.

Computer Program

A computer program is a set of data that contains instructions for the computer to follow. It tells a computer the computation it needs to work on. It retrieves the relevant data and then directs the computer with regards to which data to process. Furthermore, it *tells* the computer where to output the result of the computation(s).

The BIOS is a good example of a computer program. It is the very first thing that the computer runs when it boots. It gathers data from the hardware as input and typically displays them on the screen, in a readable format, as output.

It gives you time to provide an input from your keyboard. If it does not receive any input from you after a set period of time, it will proceed to find a suitable source of an operating system's boot file. The BIOS program and its processes are almost unnoticeable, but it happens all the time when you open a computer.

Another good example of a computer program is the calculator program on your computer or smartphone. The program waits for your input. Your input or command can either be in the form of a number, operator, or a function. Inputting the number 1, the addition operator, the number 1 again, and the equals sign will make the program instruct the computer to add the two numbers and display the result on your screen.

Most computer programs behave this way. They require input to create an output. They need data to process. Some programs may not require input from the user, but they still process data and get them from other input sources such as your computer and the programs themselves.

What Are Variables?

The computer stores the data that your program uses or will use in its RAM. To do this, the computer first finds an empty space in the RAM and allocates that space for the data your program needs. All the computer needs to do when the program and computer needs the data is to find that space and retrieve it. The name given to the specific location (within the RAM) where the data is stored is the variable. In other words, a variable is a named location of data.

Do note that the RAM is like a hotel that only offers transient lodging. The main difference is that the RAM has thousands and millions of rooms /addresses depending on its size. The computer searches for a vacant room or address when it needs to store data. The computer finds a room, gives the room number to the program, and the program instructs the computer to store the data to that room number.

This process is a relatively easy task for the computer and your computer program. However, it can be problematic for you as the computer programmer. Why? Remember that the RAM is a huge hotel with thousands and millions of rooms, and data comes in and out of it every second your computer is on.

Say that you have a text data that contains the word "Pedro". You want the program to store that information in the computer. The computer will then find space for it in the RAM.

The computer finds room 1,151,112 vacant and assigns/stores "Pedro" in it. When it is time for you to call or reference "Pedro", you need to tell the computer that you want the program to retrieve "Pedro" from room 1,151,112. Seems easy, right? Bear in mind that in programming, memory addresses are often written using hexadecimal notation (i.e. a convenient way to express binary numbers in modern computers in which a byte is almost always defined as containing eight binary digits). The room number 1,151,112 is written as 0x119088 in hexadecimal notation. This simple resource will show you how to convert a decimal to hexadecimal.

The first problem is that the RAM is a transient hotel. The location of the data you will store will be definitely in a different room number if 1,151,112 happen to be occupied when you start the program again. Memorizing the room number or address is already a difficult thing.

You might think that a good solution is to instruct the computer to find the text "Pedro", right? It seems reasonable, but what if your text data contains all the text in a Harry Potter book? You cannot type all of those in your computer program repeatedly just to find it in your computer's RAM. Also, what if your data is an image? You cannot search an image by using text.

The second problem is data duplicates. What if other programs have a text data "Pedro" as well? Things can get messy quickly if you reference data from another program. What will happen to the *other* program who actually *own* that data if you process and change that data?

The solution to the aforementioned problems is to make use of variables. **Variables have three basic components: data, identifier, and address.** You already know what data is. The address, on the other hand, is its location or address in your computer's RAM. The identifier is a letter, word, or combination of letters, numbers, and symbols, which you can use to name the address of your data.

For example, instead of memorizing the room number/address of your data, you can just tag it with a name. Say that the computer assigned the text data "Pedro" to room 1,234,456. Instead of referencing that room number to find "Pedro", you can assign an identifier to it like textName (i.e. textName = Pedro)

The computer program creates a directory of sorts, which contains pointers to your data in the memory, to make it easier for it and you to find the data in RAM. Here is a sample variable directory for a simple calculator program that is going to perform an addition operation to the numbers 12 and 436:

Identifier	Data	Memory Address
firstNumber	12	0xff456e
secondNumber	436	0x5e4775
operation	"+"	0x6f1106
result	448	0x1ca607

In older programming languages, you needed to deal with memory addresses. In modern programming languages, the compiler will handle most memory related concerns like storing and garbage collection (i.e. freeing up space in the RAM by removing unused/redundant data).

Aside from identifier, data, and addresses variables also have other components such as data type and size. Strong typed programming languages like C and Java requires programmers to declare the variable and the type of data it will contain. Stronger and stricter programming languages like Pascal require declaration of the variable and its size and type.

Python is also a strong typed language, but it does not require programmers to declare variables and its type. For example, creating a variable in Python is as simple as assigning a value or data to an identifier.

```
>>> x = 1
>>> _
```

With that simple statement, the program will create the variable x and assign a value of 1 to it. If you type the variable's identifiers in the command line, the interface will return its value.

```
>>> x
1
>>> _
```

Remember that if a variable does not exist in the program, Python or your program will return an error. For example:

```
>>> y
Traceback (most recent call last):
        File "<stdin>", line 1, in <module>
NameError: name 'y' is not defined
>>> _
```

The above error message might appear as gibberish for beginners. Fear not, later in this book, I will show you how to read and handle errors.

Naming Variables

You must remember the following rules when creating and using an identifier or name for your variable:

1. Your identifier must start with either an underscore or a letter.

2. Your identifier **must never** start with a number. The program will return an error if this occurs. Your program and Python will consider any number you type after a space as a number. You cannot use a number as an identifier. Your numbers cannot contain letters or symbols except when writing in a different numeric notation (e.g., hexadecimal 0x12E4).

3. Your identifier must only contain letters, numbers, and underscores.

4. Your identifier is case sensitive. This means that identifier X is different from identifier x.

5. Your identifier can be as short as 1 character (e.g., x, _, y, etc.).

6. Your identifier must not be the same as a keyword (these are reserved words e.g. return, True, False etc.) or a function.

Not following or adhering to these simple rules may lead to errors or unintended results in your program.

Using Variables

The primary function of variables is to store data. Storing data in a variable is as simple as using the assignment operator (=). Here is an example:

```
>>> x = 1
>>> _
```

In the example, the lines of codes created the variable x and assigned the number 1 to it. Assigning a variable is like Algebra. The assignment statement reads x is equal to 1. It can also be read as x has a value of 1 or 1 is assigned to x.

You can also assign the value of a variable to another variable. For example:

```
>>> a = 10
>>> b = a
>>> b
10
>>> _
```

There are other ways of assigning data to variables. One of them is assigning the result of an expression or operation to a variable, which will be discussed later.

Naming Conventions

You can easily get errors by being too careless with the identifiers you create. For one, you can receive an error by using variable THIS_IS_A_VARIABLE instead of this_is_a_variable. To prevent variable naming errors, you must follow or create your own naming convention. As a beginner, you should follow these tips first as your guide in creating identifiers.

Naming by Description

The best practice when it comes to naming variables is to name it using its description. Descriptions are memorable and descriptive words are easier to type than just typing random combination of letters or words. Also, other people who will look at your code can easily understand the context, purpose, and data type of your variables with description.

For example:

```
>>> christmas = "December 25"
>>> name = "John Doe"
```

```
>>> age = 25
>>> _
```

This kind of naming style is simple but can easily go out of hand quick. Remember that you can use one-word identifier or description when your program is still small. Bigger programs or projects can easily force you to create long identifiers and descriptions. Why? For one, this is to avoid different variables having the same identifier. Second, it makes variable management easier.

Here are some variable naming scenarios that you will encounter along the way.

Scenario 1:

```
>>> employeename1 = "Garett Jones"
>>> employeename1 = "John Doe"
>>> _
```

Scenario 2:

```
>>> firstname = "John"
>>> lastname = "Doe"
>>> _
```

In these scenarios where you are forced to use more than one word for descriptions, you need to establish how you arrange and present them. One of the most common naming conventions that programmers use in these kinds of scenarios is Camel Case typing.

For example:

```
>>> employeeName1 = "Garett Jones"
>>> employeeName2 = "John Doe"
>>> _
```

Scenario 2:

```
>>> firstName = "John"
>>> lastName = "Doe"
>>> _
```

Another convention is to use underscores.

```
>>> employee_name_1 = "Garett Jones"
>>> employee_name_2 = "John Doe"
>>> _
```

Scenario 2:

```
>>> first_name = "John"
>>> last_name = "Doe"
>>> _
```

You must enforce uniformity when working with multiple word identifiers or descriptions. You must create a naming structure to make the names more organized, memorable, and easier to type. A rule of thumb is to write the description in this format: noun/object + adjective/property + adverb.

For example:

```
>>> employee1_name_first = "John"
>>> employee2_name_last = "Doe"
>>> _
```

Of course, this is just a naming convention. It is not a rule, but it does help in organizing your variables. Also, most of the scenarios listed in this section can be solved by taking advantage of arrays, objects, and classes. Most of those will be discussed much later in this book.

Another scenario that you will encounter has to do with variables having the same description but different data types.

For example:

```
>>> employee_number = "emp-107012005"
>>> employee_number = 107012005
>>> _
```

What you can do is to add prefixes on your variables.

For example:

```
>>> str_employee_number = "emp-107012005"
>>> int_employee_number = 107012005
>>> _
```

Data types will be discussed later.

There are multiple naming conventions that you can use or apply in your programs. You can even create one of your own if you like. However, if you have other people working with you and your program, it is best that you set the naming convention standard for your project.

Introduction to Expressions and Python Operators

At this point, you already know how to store and access data in your program. The next part is processing them. Programming languages have operators. They can manipulate and process data. You code expressions when using operators.

Expressions

Expressions are lines of codes that perform operations using operators, which the program or computer evaluates to return a result. The term expression in programming is like Algebraic expressions wherein you have variables or data placed on the left and right side of an operator. For example, 1 + 2 is an expression.

Expressions have multiple components. They are constants, variables, data, operators, delimiters, parentheses, functions, and results or output. In the expression 1 + 2, 1 and 2 are data, + is the operator, and 3 is the output.

There are multiple types of expressions. Some of them are arithmetic, relational/comparison, Boolean/logical, string, bitwise, and mixed expressions. The type of expression you create depends on the operators you use and the data type of your expected result.

Your program is all about expressions. Expression mostly dictates the processing of data in your program. You can also use it in different scenarios. And one of the most common scenarios is to assign an output of an expression to a variable.

Example 1:

```
>>> x = 1 + 2
>>> x
3
>>> _
```

Example 2:

```
>>> operandFirst = 1
>>> operandSecond = 2
>>> output = operandFirst + operandSecond
>>> output
3
>>> _
```

Operators

Python, just like many other programming languages, have numerous operators like arithmetic operators addition (+), subtraction (-), multiplication (*), and division (/). Some of those operators have similar functionalities in most programing languages.

Operators are divided according to their functionality and the data type of expression or output that they produce. Most operators use signs and symbols while some use keywords. Some operators that perform uncommon or advanced data processing use functions.

Note that not adding space between operands and operators will work. However, it is best that you avoid typing expressions like that to prevent any potential syntax errors.

Arithmetic Operators

Operation	Operator	Description	Example

Addition	+	Adds numbers	>>> 1 + 1
			2
			>>> _

Subtraction	-	Subtracts numbers	>>> 10 - 12
			-2
			>>> _

Multiplication	*	Multiplies numbers	>>> 42 * 35
			1470
			>>> _

Division	/	Divides the left-hand number by the right-hand number	>>> 132 / 11
			12
			>>> _

Floor Division	//	Divides the left-hand number by the right-hand number and returns only the whole number, effectively removing any decimal value, from the quotient	>>> 10 // 3
			3
			>>> _

Modulus	%	Performs a floor division on the left-hand number by the right-hand number and returns the remainder	>>> 133 / 11
			1
			>>> _

Exponent	**	Raises the left-hand number by the right-hand power	>>> 4 ** 2
			16
			>>> _

Relational Operators

Operation	Operator	Description	Example

Is Equal to	==	Returns true if left and right hand sides are equal	>>> 999 == 999
			True
			>>> _

Is Not Equal to	!=	Returns true if left and right hand sides are not equal	>>> 24 != 123
			True
			>>> _

Is Greater Than	>	Returns true if left-hand side's value is greater than the right-hand's side	>>> 554 > 64
			True
			>>> _

Is Less Than	<	Returns true if left-hand side's value is lesser than the right-hand's side	>>> 16 < 664
			True
			>>> _

Is Equal or Greater Than	>=	Returns true if left-hand side's value is greater or equal than the right-hand's side	>>> 554 >= 64
			True
			>>> 554 >= 554
			True
			>>> _

Is Equal or Less Than	<=	Returns true if left-hand side's value is lesser or equal than the right-hand's side	>>> 16 <= 664
			True
			>>> 16 <= 16
			True
			>>> _

Assignment Operator

Operation	Operator	Description	Example

Assign	=	Assigns the value of the right-hand operand to the variable on the left	>>> x = 1
			>>> x
			1
			>>> _

Add and Assign	+=	Adds the value of the left variable and the value of the right-hand operand and assign the result to the left variable	>>> x = 14
			>>> x
			14
			>>> x += 16
			>>> x
			30
			>>> _

Subtract and Assign	-=	Subtracts the value of the left variable and the value of the right-hand operand and assign the result to the left variable	>>> x = 30
			>>> x
			30
			>>> x -= 4
			>>> x
			26

			>>> _

Multiply and Assign	*=	Multiplies the value of the left variable and the value of the right-hand operand and assign the result to the left variable	>>> x = 26
			>>> x
			26
			>>> x *= 10
			>>> x
			260
			>>> _

Divide and Assign	/=	Divides the value of the left variable by the value of the right-hand operand and assign the result to the left variable	>>> x = 260
			>>> x
			260
			>>> x /= 13
			>>> x
			20
			>>> _

Floor Divide and Assign	//=	Performs a floor division on the value of the left variable by the value of the right-hand operand and assign the quotient as a whole number to the left variable	>>> x = 20
			>>> x
			20
			>>> x //= 3
			>>> x
			6
			>>> _

Modulus and Assign	%=	Performs a floor division on the value of the left variable by the value of the right-hand operand and assign the remainder of the quotient to the left variable	>>> x = 6
			>>> x
			6
			>>> x %= 4
			>>> x
			2
			>>> _

Exponent/Raise and Assign	%=	Raises the value of the left variable by the power of the value of the right-hand operand and assign the result to the left variable	>>> x = 2
			>>> x
			2
			>>> x **= 3
			>>> x
			8
			>>> _

Logical Operators

Operation	Operator	Description	Example
Logical And	and	Returns true if both of the operands	>>> True and True

		are true	True
			>>> _
Logical Or	or	Returns true if at least one of the operands is true	>>> True or False
			True
			>>> _
Logical Not	NOT	Returns the negated logical state of the operand	>>> not True
			False
			>>> _

Truth Table

The operator *and* will only return True if both of the operands are True. It will always return False otherwise. The operator *or* will only return False if both operands are False. Otherwise, it will always return True. The operator *not* will return False if the operand is True and will return True if the operand is False.

Below are truth tables for operator 'and' and 'or'.

Left Operand	Logical Operator	Right Operand	Result
True	And	True	True
True		False	False
False		True	False
False		False	False

Left Operand	Logical Operator	Right Operand	Result
True	or	True	True
True		False	True
False		True	True
False		False	False

Membership Operators

Operation	Operator	Description	Example
In	In	Returns True if left operand's value is present in the value of the right operand	>>> x = "cat and dog"
			>>> a = "cat"
			>>> b = "dog"
			>>> c = "mouse"
			>>> a in x
			True
			>>> b in x

			True
			>>> c in x
			False
			>>> _
Not In	not in	Returns true if left operand's value is not present in the value of the right operand	>>> x = "cat and dog"
			>>> a = "cat"
			>>> b = "dog"
			>>> c = "mouse"
			>>> a not in x
			False
			>>> b not in x
			False
			>>> c not in x
			True
			>>> _

Identity Operators

Operation	Operator	Description	Example

Is	is	Returns True if left operand's identity is the same with the identity of the right operand
		
		Note: If may appear that it returns True if the values of the operands are equal, but Python evaluates the identity or ID and not the values.
		
		Equal values of a single data or variable tend to receive similar IDs. Results of expressions may receive new IDs or overlap with existing IDs with similar values.
		
		To check the ID of variables and data, you need to use the id() keyword/function.
		
		If you want to compare if values of the operands are equal, use ==
			>>> x = "a"
			>>> id(x)
			34232504
			>>> id("a")
			34232504
			>>> x is "a"
			True
			>>> x * 2
			'aa'
			>>> x * 2 is "aa"
			False
			>>> id(x * 2)
			39908384
			>>> id("aa")
			39908552
			>>> x * 2 is 2 * x
			False
			>>> id(x * 2)
			39908552
			>>> id(2 * x)
			39908384

		operator instead.	>>> _

Is Not	is not	Returns True if left operand's identity is not the same with the identity of the right operand	>>> x = "a"
			>>> id(x)
			34232504
			>>> id("a")
			34232504
			>>> x is not "a"
			False
			>>> x * 2
			'aa'
			>>> x * 2 is not "aa"
			True
			>>> _

Bitwise Operators

Operation	Operator	Description	Example

Bitwise And (AND)	&	Returns 1 for bits if both operands have 1 on the same place value. Returns 0 for 0-0, 1-0, and 0-1 combinations.	>>> 0b1101 & 0b1001
			9
			>>> bin(9)
			'0b1001'
			>>> _

Bitwise Or (OR)	|	Returns 0 for bits if both operands have 0 on the same place value. Returns 1 for 1-1, 1-0, and 0-1 combinations.	>>> 0b1101 | 0b1001
			13
			>>> bin(13)
			'0b1101'
			>>> _

Bitwise Exclusive Or (XOR)	^	Returns 1 for bits if both operands have 0 and 1 on the same place value. Returns 0 for 1-1 and 0-0 combinations.	>>> 0b1101 ^ 0b1001
			4
			>>> bin(4)
			'0b100'
			>>> _

Bitwise Complement	~	Flips each bit and negates the value	>>> ~0b1010
			-11
			>>> bin(-11)
			'-0b1011

			>>> _

Bitwise Left Shift	<<	Moves bits of the left operand to left. The number of shifting of bits is according to the value of the right operand.	>>> 0b1010 << 2
			40
			>>> bin(40)
			'0b101000'
			>>> _

Bitwise Left Shift	>>	Moves bits of the left operand to right. The number of shifting of bits is according to the value of the right operand.	>>> 0b1010 >> 2
			2
			>>> bin(2)
			'0b10'
			>>> _

Below are truth tables for operator 'and', 'or', and 'xor'.

Left Operand	Logical Operator	Right Operand	Result
1		1	1
1	&	0	0
0		1	0
0		0	0

Left Operand	Logical Operator	Right Operand	Result
1		1	1
1	|	0	1
0		1	1
0		0	0

Left Operand	Logical Operator	Right Operand	Result
1		1	0
1	^	0	1
0		1	1
0		0	0

Practice Exercise

Create code for the following scenarios.

1. Create 5 separate expressions that will lead to a result of 10025. You cannot use an arithmetic operator more than once and your first number must be 7.

2. Find the statistical mean of 10 survey respondents' ages. The ages are 18, 21, 19, 52, 6, 33, 15, 46, 72, and 25.

3. Find the value of x using these details:

    a. x = y + (a * b / c)

    b. y = a + 151

    c. b = c * (144 + y)

    d. y = 10

    e. c = 7

4. Johnny was born on February 14, 1967. How many days old was he on January 1, 2000?

5. A car was moving 20 miles per hour on a straight road. Every five minutes, it instantly decelerates by 5 miles per hour and keeps that speed for a minute and then instantly accelerates back to 20 miles per hour. How many miles will the car cover if it moves like that for an hour?

Chapter Summary

Throughout your programming career, you will deal with variables and operators. They are the core elements in a program. After all, programs are all about data. Without variables, it will be difficult to keep track and process data. In fact, without operators your program will not process anything.

The more operators you know, the more versatile your program will be. However, it does not mean that you will always use all the operators in your program.

Remember that you do not need to force yourself to use complicated operations just because they make your program look complex. If a regular operator can get you the results you need, use it. Always prioritize simplicity over complexity and aesthetics.

When it comes to identifiers, always make sure that they are contextual. Your variables' purpose and content should be easily known by just reading their identifiers. Even people who are not working on your program or who do not know how to program should be able to identify your variables.

Congratulations on your progress so far! Now that you know how to process data and where to keep them, it is time for you to know the types of data which are available in Python and you can use in your program.

Chapter 2: Solution

Question 1

```
>>> 7 * 1432
10024
>>> 7 + 10017
10024
>>> 7 - -10017
10024
>>> 7 / 0.0006983240223463687
10024.0
>>> 7 // 0.0006983
10024.0
>>> _
```

Question 2

```
>>> (18 + 21 + 19 + 52 + 6 + 33 + 15 + 46 + 72 + 25) / 10
30.7
>>> _
```

Question 3

```
>>> c = 7
>>> y = 10
>>> b = c * (144 + y)
>>> b
1078
>>> a = y - 151
>>> a
-141
>>> x = y + (a * b / c)
>>> x
-21704.0
>>> _
```

Question 4

To solve this question, we need to find out the *difference* (in days) between January 1, 2000 and February 14, 1967. There are 33 years counting from year 1967 to year 2000. In order to convert to days we need to multiply this with 365.25.

In addition, there are 44 days between January 1 and February 14. That is from January 1 to January 31 is a total of 30 days. We then have an additional 14 days in February.

Therefore:

```
>>> ((2000 - 1967) * 365.25) - 44)
12009.25
>>> _
```

Question 5

Let us begin with what we know.

The car travelled in two phases. In phase 1, it travelled at 20 miles per hour for 5 minutes (1/12hr). In the second phase, it travelled at 15 miles per hour (after 5 miles per hour deceleration) for one minute (1/60hr).

Duration is the amount of time spent in a given phase. From the question, we know that duration1 is 5 times duration 2.

Since the speed and deceleration is in miles per hour, we convert all the time spent in each phase from minute(s) to hour for uniformity sake. Hence 5 minutes is 1/12hr etc.

The car travelled for a total of 1 hour hence totalTime = 1

Therefore, we have the below:

```
>>> totalTime = 1
>>> time1 = 1/12
>>> time2 = 1/60
>>> speed1 = 20
>>> deceleration = 5
>>> speed2 = speed1 - deceleration
>>> duration1 = totalTime*((time1)/ (time1 + time2))
>>> duration2 = totalTime*((time2)/(time1 + time2))
>>> distance1 = speed1 * duration1
>>> distance2 = speed2 * duration2
>>> totalDistance = distance1 + distance2
>>> totalDistance
19.166666666666668
>>> _
```

Ever wondered why it's called Python?

There's an interesting story about it. While implementing Python, Van Rossum was also reading the published scripts from "Monty Python's Flying Circus", a BBC comedy series in the 1970s. Since he wanted a short, unique and slightly mysterious name for his invention, he got inspired by the series and named it Python!

Chapter 3

Simple Data Types

I can't stress enough the fact that computer programs revolve around data. Because of this, you should endeavor to master the types of data that you will encounter and use in Python programming.

Before anything else, familiarize yourself with the term literals. Literals are pieces of data that are written plainly in your program code. For example:

```
>>> x = 1
>>> y = "This is a string literal"
>>> _
```

The number (on line 1) is a *numeric* literal and the words enclosed in the quotes (on line 2) are *string* literals.

Numbers

In Python, there are four types of number data types. They are integers, long, float, and complex.

Signed Integers:

Integers (int), or signed integers, are whole numbers. Its value ranges from negative numbers to 0 to positive numbers. Basically, they are numbers without a decimal point. Integers have a numerical limit. If the value of the integer goes beyond a certain limit, the data type of the integer transforms into a long integer.

Long Integers:

Long integers (long) are also whole numbers similar to signed integers. The only difference is that long integers do not have a numerical limit. Note that all integers in Python 3 are now long by default i.e. what was *long* in Python 2 is now the standard *int* type in Python 3.

Floating Point Real Values:

Floating point real values (floats) represent real numbers. They are written with a decimal point dividing the integer and fractional parts. Floats can be written using the usual method of typing in numbers:

```
>>> float (2)
>>> 2.0
>>> _
```

or it can be written using scientific notation that includes the usage of **e** in the number.

```
>>> 2.5e2
>>> 250.0
>>> _
```

Complex Numbers:

A complex number is a number that can be expressed in the form a + b*i*, where a and b are real numbers and *i* is a solution of the equation x^2 = -1. Because no real number satisfies this equation, *i* is called an imaginary or irrational number. For the complex number, a + bi, a is called the real part and b is called the imaginary part.

An example of an irrational number is the square root of 2. Since the square root of 2 does not provide an exact numerical value, it is much better to use it in form of an irrational number or imaginary number.

String

Strings are combination of numbers, letters, and symbols enclosed within quotations. Remember that anything outside quotation marks is treated as identifiers, keywords, numbers, or operators. You can use either single or double quotes to enclose strings.

For example:

```
>>> x = "This is a string"
>>> x
'This is a string'
>>> _
```

Combining/Concatenating strings

You can combine or concatenate strings using the addition operator (+).

For example:

```
>>> y = "This is "
>>> z = "a string."
>>> x = y + z
>>> x
'This is a string.'
>>> _
```

Avoiding Type Errors with Conversion Functions

Dealing with multiple data types can be confusing for beginners. For example, do you consider "2" as a number? If you say yes, then you will tend to receive a lot of datatype error. For example:

```
>>> 2 + "2"
```

```
Traceback (most recent call last):
  File "<stdin>", line 1, in <module>
TypeError: unsupported operand type(s) for +: 'int' and 'str'
>>> _
```

As you can see in the error message, the second operand was considered as a "str" or string. Always remember that most operations will work as intended if you use the appropriate data type.

However, there will be times that you will receive input that are of a different type. For example:

```
>>> 2 + input()
2
Traceback (most recent call last):
  File "<stdin>", line 1, in <module>
TypeError: unsupported operand type(s) for +: 'int' and 'str'
>>> x = input()
2
>>> x
'2'
>>> _
```

The keyword input() makes the shell ask for something to be typed on the command line from the user. As you can see, the number 2 was input without quotes, but when its value was checked, it was converted to a string.

You can mitigate this by using conversion functions. For example:

```
>>> 2 + int(input())
2
4
>>> x = int(input())
2
>>> x
2
>>> _
```

The example used the int() function to convert literals to integers. Note the word literals. The int() function does not only convert strings, but it also converts other data types. For example:

```
>>> int(23.5412341231)
23
>>> int(True)
1
>>> int(False)
0
```

```
>>> _
```

Another handy function that convert data types is str(). As it name implies, it converts literals to strings. For example:

```
>>> str(2)
'2'
>>> str(251.12312)
'251.12312'
>>> str(True)
'True'
>>> str(False)
'False'
>>> _
```

There are other functions that can be used for data type conversion such as float(), hex(), bin(), and bool(). You can easily guess the data types they result to by their identifiers alone.

Avoiding, Replacing, and Stripping Whitespace

Considering whitespace as a problem is a debatable topic. Whitespaces are tabs, new lines, leading and trailing spaces.

There are two instances where they can be considered an issue: inside a string and within your code. Be that as it may, they are mostly trivial and not code breaking.

Trailing spaces (trailing space is all whitespace located at the end of a line) from input data often is not a problem caused by programmers but mostly users and other input sources. For example, if you are using Python to create a program to handle server side scripts, it will often encounter inputs that contain trailing whitespace (e.g., HTML text).

To remove both trailing and leading spaces, You can use the strip() method of the string class. For example:

```
>>> x = "    This    is   spaced      badly.    "
>>> x.strip()
'This    is   spaced      badly.'
>>> _
```

Note – the internal spaces are preserved.

If the problem is trailing spaces, you can use rstrip() to get rid of it. Conversely, you can lstrip() to get rid of just the leading space.

```
>>> x = "    This    is   spaced      badly.    "
>>> x.rstrip()
'    This    is   spaced      badly.'
```

```
>>> _
```

```
>>> x = "    This      is    spaced       badly.      "
>>> x.lstrip()
'This    is    spaced       badly.     '
>>> _
```

Another way to remove both the leading and trailing space is to nest the methods together:

```
>>> x = "    This      is    spaced       badly.      "
>>> x.strip().rstrip()
'This    is    spaced       badly.'
>>> _
```

Or you can do it this way:

```
>>> x = "    This      is    spaced       badly.      "
>>> (x.strip()).rstrip()
'This    is    spaced       badly.'
>>> _
```

Note that strip() and rstrip() also remove leading and trailing tabs and new line characters.

```
>>> x = "\t    This      is    spaced       badly.    \n"
>>> x.strip()
'This    is    spaced       badly.'
>>> x.rstrip()
'\t    This    is    spaced       badly.'
>>> _
```

Note that \t and \n are escape character combination for tab and new line respectively. These combinations start with the escape character "\"Escape character combinations help you input irregular characters into your strings such as tabs and new line characters.

It also allows you to type in characters that may pose a problem when you just plainly type them on your keyboard such as \\, \r, \", and \'. For example:

```
>>> print("\tHello\nWorld!\n\"This is another way to type quotes\"")
    Hello
World!
"This is another way to type quotes"
>>> _
```

How can you remove the repeating spaces in the middle of the string? You can use the replace() method for that. For example:

```
>>> x = "   This   is   spaced   badly.   "
>>> x.replace("  ", "")
' This is spaced badly. '
>>> _
```

The replace() method was used to replace two spaces with an empty string. Basically, it will progressively remove all the two spaces until single spaces remains.

Avoiding syntax errors with strings

The primary method of avoiding syntax errors when working with strings is to make sure that you have properly enclosed the string inside a pair of quotation marks.

Improper String:

```
>>> x = "This is a string.'
  File "<stdin>", line 1
    x = "This is a string.'
                          ^
SyntaxError: EOL while scanning string literal.
>>> _
```

Proper String:

```
>>> x = "This is a string."
>>> x
'This is a string.'
>>> _
```

Note that you should close a double quotation mark with a double quotation mark, and close a single quotation mark with a single quotation mark. Here is another example:

Improper String:

```
>>> x = "Then Mark said, "Don't you dare touch that!""
  File "<stdin>", line 1
    x = "Then Mark said, "Don't you dare touch that!""
                        ^
SyntaxError: EOL while scanning string literal
>>> _
```

If your string has a quotation mark, enclose it with a different quotation mark. For example:

```
>>> x = 'Then Mark said, "Don't you dare touch that!"'
  File "<stdin>", line 1
    x = 'Then Mark said, "Don't you dare touch that!"'
                                ^
SyntaxError: EOL while scanning string literal
>>> _
```

The previous example should have worked, but remember that the word "don't" uses a single quotation mark, which basically made the interpreter think that the single quote ended the string literal. If you take the single quote out, the statement will work.

```
>>> x = 'Then Mark said, "Dont you dare touch that!"'
>>> x
'Then Mark said, "Dont you dare touch that!"'
>>> _
```

The simple rule is to not use the quotation mark you used to enclose the string to prevent errors.

The previous solution worked, but it ruined your intended value. If you need to use both types of quotation marks, you can use concatenation. For example:

```
>>> x = 'Then Mark said, "'
>>> y = "Don't you dare touch that!"
>>> z = x + y + '"'
>>> z
'Then Mark said, "Don't you dare touch that!"'
>>> _
```

Collections/Sequences

A collection or a sequence is a collection of literals or data in a variable. In other programming languages, it can be considered as an array. There are four types of arrays or collections in Python.

1. List
2. Tuple
3. Set
4. Dictionary

List

A list is a collection that is ordered and changeable. It also allows duplicate members. The comma separator separates the pieces of data or literals assigned to a list. Here is a simple example of a list:

```
>>> sampleList = ["Data 1", "Data 2", "Data 3"]
>>> sampleList
['Data 1', 'Data 2', 'Data 3']
>>> _
```

Each data included in the list receives an index according to its position in the assignment. The index starts with 0. In the example, "Data 1" will receive an index of 0, "Data 2" will receive an index of 1, and "Data 3" will receive an index of 2.

You can assign numbers, strings, or a mix of literals in a list. For example:

```
>>> sampleList = ["Data 1", 11241, 0b101101]
>>> sampeList
['Data 1', 11241, 45]
>>> _
```

Accessing elements in a list

To access an element or entry in a list, you can just type the name of the list identifiers together with a pair of square brackets containing the index of the data you want to access. For example:

```
>>> sampleList = ["Data 1", 11241, 0b101101]
>>> sampleList[0]
'Data 1'
>>> sampleList[1]
11241
>>> sampleList[2]
45
>>> _
```

Index positions

Keep in mind that using a negative index will result in you accessing the list elements in reverse. The last element in the list will have the index of -1, and so on. For example:

Note - 0b101101 is the binary representation of 45

```
>>> sampleList = ["Data 1", 11241, 0b101101]
>>> sampleList[-1]
45
>>> sampleList[-2]
```

```
11241
>>> sampleList[-3]
'Data 1'
>>> _
```

Using individual values from a list

You can assign an individual value from a list to a variable. For example:

```
>>> sampleList = ["This is a string", 1, 2, 3]
>>> x = sampleList[0]
>>> x
'This is a string'
>>> _
```

You can access multiple list items in a sequence by using the colon or slice (:) operator. The left hand side of the colon indicates the starting index of the sequence and the right hand side of the colon indicates where the slice stops. For example:

```
>>> sampleList = ["Data 1", 11241, 0b101101]
>>> sampleList[1:3]
[11241, 45]
>>> _
```

Changing, Adding and Removing Elements

Changing the value of an item in the list can easily be achieved by assigning a value to it. For example:

```
>>> sampleList = ["This will be changed", 1, 2, 3]
>>> sampleList[0]
'This will be changed'
>>> sampleList[0] = "This is a new string"
>>> sampleList[0]
'This is a new string'
>>> sampleList
['This is a new string', 1, 2, 3]
>>> _
```

Adding an element to a list is as simple as using the addition or concatenate (+) operator. For example:

```
>>> sampleList = [1, 2, 3, 4]
>>> sampleList = sampleList + [5]
>>> sampleList
[1, 2, 3, 4, 5]
>>> _
```

An alternative way to do this is to use the assign and add/concatenate (+=) operator.

```
>>> sampleList = [1, 2, 3, 4]
>>> sampleList += [5]
>>> sampleList
[1, 2, 3, 4, 5]
>>> _
```

Deleting an item inside a list requires the use of the del keyword and accessing the item that you want to be deleted. For example:

```
>>> sampleList = [1, 2, 3]
>>> del sampleList[0]
>>> sampleList
[2, 3]
>>> _
```

Note that when you delete an item in the list, the index of all that items that comes after its position will be shifted left. In the previous example, since you delete the item 0 that contains the value, the items with the index 1 and 2 will become index 0 and 1. So if you access index 0, the program will return the value of 2.

If you do not want that to happen, you can leave and just ignore the value of the item or you can just set it to zero or blank if the value is a string. For example:

```
>>> sampleList = ["This is a string", 1, 2, 3]
>>> sampleList[0] = ""
>>> sampleList[1] = 0
>>> sampleList
["", 0, 2, 3]
>>> _
```

Another way of removing an item from the list is using the remove() method. For example:

```
>>> sampleList = [1, 2, 3]
>>> sampleList.remove(1)
>>> sampleList
[2, 3]
>>> _
```

Note that the remove() method removes the item, with the lowest index, of the same value that was used as an argument in the parentheses. For example:

```
>>> sampleList = [1, 2, 3, 1, 1, 1]
>>> sampleList.remove(1)
```

```
>>> sampleList
[2, 3, 1, 1, 1]
>>> _
```

List Operations, Expressions, and Methods

Remember that everything in Python is an object. This means that lists have their innate methods. They also behave as strings, which means they can use string operations such as concatenation. To find out what an object's innate methods and attributes are, you can use the dir function. For example:

```
>>> sampleList = [1, 2, 3, 4, 5]
>>> dir(sampleList)
['__add__', '__class__', '__contains__', '__delattr__', '__delitem__', '__dir__', '__doc__', '__eq__', '__format__', '__ge__', '__getattribute__', '__getitem__', '__gt__', '__hash__', '__iadd__', '__imul__', '__init__', '__init_subclass__', '__iter__', '__le__', '__len__', '__lt__', '__mul__', '__ne__', '__new__', '__reduce__', '__reduce_ex__', '__repr__', '__reversed__', '__rmul__', '__setattr__', '__setitem__', '__sizeof__', '__str__', '__subclasshook__', 'append', 'clear', 'copy', 'count', 'extend', 'index', 'insert', 'pop', 'remove', 'reverse', 'sort']
>>> _
```

A few of the important methods you will frequently use with lists are: *sort*, *reverse* and *count*.

A few of the important built-in functions that you will frequently use with lists are: *sorted*, *reversed*, and *len*.

Sorting a list permanently

To sort a list permanently, you need to use list's sort() method. For example:

```
>>> numberList = [5, 4, 3, 2, 1]
>>> numberList.sort()
>>> numberList
[1, 2, 3, 4, 5]
>>> _
```

Sorting a list temporarily

To sort a list temporarily, you need to use the built-in function sorted(). For example:

```
>>> numberList = [5, 4, 3, 2, 1]
>>> sorted(numberList)
[1, 2, 3, 4, 5]
>>> _
```

Printing a list in reverse order

Returning a reversed order of a list temporarily is a bit tricky. To do this, you will need to perform a slice. For example

```
>>> numberList = [1, 2, 3, 4, 5]
>>> numberList[::-1]
[5, 4, 3, 2, 1]
>>> _
```

Note that this only reverses the order of the items in the list. It does not perform a sort. Here is another example:

```
>>> numberList = [7, 6, 4, 2, 1, 8]
>>> numberList[::-1]
[8, 1, 2, 4, 6, 7]
>>> _
```

Finding the length of a list

To find the length of a list, you can use the built-in function len(). For example:

```
>>> numberList = [5, 4, 3, 2, 1]
>>> len(numberList)
5
>>> _
```

Avoiding Index Errors when working with lists

To avoid index errors when working with lists, you must remember these:

1. The total count of items in the list. You can always remind yourself and your program about the total count by using len().

2. Lists are zero based. The index always starts with 0.

3. Removing and adding an item on the list always change the total count. Changing the data of an item does not.

Working with Lists

Lists have multiple purposes in programming. For one, lists are an excellent way to reduce the amount of variables you need to create. For example:

```
>>> x = 135
>>> y = 247
>>> z = 359
>>> total1 = x + y + z
>>> total1
741
```

```
>>> a = [135, 247, 359]
>>> total2 = sum(a)
>>> total2
741
>>> _
```

The example only deals with three values and shows two different ways you can process them. As you can see, assigning them in a list instead of assigning them to separate variables is a much easier and faster way to process those values.

The example might only show little advantage, but think about a scenario wherein you need to deal with 20 or more pieces of data.

On the other hand, lists are useful when receiving an inconsistent amount of data during runtime. Instead of preparing a set amount of variables ready to receive those data, you can just use a list since lists can hold unspecified number of values.

Looping through an entire list

Another advantage of lists against other regular data types and variables is that you can loop through them with ease. Here is the previous example with the addition of a loop method to work with a list:

```
>>> x = 135
>>> y = 247
>>> z = 359
>>> total1 = x + y + z
>>> total1
741
>>> a = [135, 247, 359]
>>> total2 = a[0] + a[1] + a[2]
>>> total2
741
>>> total3 = 0
>>> for i in range(len(a)):
...     total3 += a[i]
...
>>> total3
741
>>> _
```

There are two common ways to loop through a list. The first method is using the "for" loop together with the range() and len() functions. The second method is to use while loop and the len() function.

```
>>> a = [135, 247, 359]
>>> total1 = 0
>>> for i in range(len(a)):
...     total1 += a[i]
...
>>> total1
741
>>> total2 = 0
>>> while (i < len(a)):
...     total2 += a[i]
...     i += 1
...
>>> _
```

Since list indices are incremental in nature, you can use loop counters, which also increments per loop, as list indices to scan through a list.

Currently, the simplest and popular method is to use *for* and *in* combination without using range() and len(). For example:

```
>>> a = [135, 247, 359]
>>> total1 = 0
>>> for item in a:
...     total1 += item
...
>>> total1
741
```

However, this method does not give you easier control with regards to picking the items you only need. For example, if you only want to use the value of the a[0] and a[1], you cannot do that without using a loop counter or index.

For example:

```
>>> a = [135, 247, 359]
>>> total1 = 0
>>> for i in range(len(a)):
...     if (i == 1):
...         continue
...     total1 += a[i]
...
>>> total1
494
```

Another method to loop through a list is to use list iteration object. The iteration object allows you to navigate through your list item by item using the built-in function next(). For example:

```
>>> a = [135, 247, 359]
>>> b = iter(a)
>>> next(b)
135
>>> next(b)
247
>>> next(b)
359
>>> c = iter(a)
>>> for i in range(len(a)):
...     print(next(c))
...
135
247
359
>>> _
```

Loops will be discussed in-depth in the next chapter.

Avoiding indentation errors

For convenience, Python allows developers to assign items to a list in multiple lines. For example:

```
>>> sampleList = [
    1,
    2,
    3,
    4
    ]
>>> sampleList
[1, 2, 3, 4]
>>> _
```

You can even do this:

```
>>> sampleList = [
    1
    ,2,
    3
    ,4]
>>> sampleList
[1, 2, 3, 4]
```

```
>>> _
```

This can also be done within a code block and it disregards the indentation level:

```
>>> def randomFunction():
>>>     sampleList = [
    1
    ,2,
    3
    ,4]
    print(sampleList)
>>> randomFunction()
[1, 2, 3, 4]
>>> _
```

However, even if you can do this, do not. You can encounter indentation errors doing things this way. Nonetheless, it does not mean that this "feature" is useless. You can use this technique if the individual items within the list use a lot of horizontal space.

For example:

```
>>> sampleList = [
    "However, even if you can do this, do not.",
    "You can encounter indentation errors doing things this way.",
    "Nonetheless, it does not mean that this "\feature\" is useless.",
    "Do this if the items take a lot of horizontal space."
]

>>> _
```

Displaying enumerated lists

If you want to display an enumerated list, you can use the enumerate() function. The function allows you to parse through the list, get both index and value, and assign them to variables in the loop statement. For example:

```
>>> a = [135, 247, 359]
>>> for i, item in enumerate(a):
    print(str(i) + ". " + str(item))
0. 135
1. 247
2. 359
>>> _
```

Since the example is using the concatenation operator, it is important that you convert all the numbers into string to make sure you will not receive a TypeError exception.

Tuple

Tuples are sequences, just like lists. You can assign multiple items or values in it. And you can access its items using indices enclosed in square brackets.

However, the main difference between a tuple and a list is that tuples are immutable. This means that you *cannot* change the number of items it contains or alter their values.

Also, instead of using square brackets to contain items, it uses parentheses. For example:

```
>>> sampleList = [1, 2, 3, 4]
>>> sampleList
[1, 2, 3, 4]
>>> sampleTuple = (1, 2, 3, 4)
>>> sampleTuple
(1, 2, 3, 4)
>>> sampleTuple[0]
1
>>> sampleTuple[1]
2
>>> sampleTuple[2]
3
>>> sampleTuple[3]
4
>>> sampleTuple[0] = 10
Traceback (most recent call last):
  File "<stdin>", line 1, in <module>
TypeError: 'tuple' object does not support item assignment
>>> i = iter(sampleTuple)
>>> next(i)
1
>>> next(i)
2
>>> next(i)
3
>>> next(i)
4
>>> _
```

Another difference between a tuple and a list is that assigning a single item in a tuple requires a comma. For example:

```
>>> sampleTuple = (1,)
>>> sampleTuple
(1,)
>>> _
```

The reason for this is the inclusion of parentheses. If you remove the comma, the value will be considered a value inside parentheses as if you are writing an expression.

```
>>> sampleTuple = (1)
>>> sampleTuple == 1
True
>>> type(sampleTuple)
(class 'int')
>>> sampleTuple[0]
Traceback (most recent call last):
  File "<stdin>", line 1, in <module>
TypeError: 'int' object is not subscriptable
>>> sampleTuple = (1,)
>>> sampleTuple == 1
False
>>> type(sampleTuple)
(class 'tuple')
>>> sampleTuple[0]
1
>>> sampleTuple = ("text")
>>> sampleTuple == "text"
True
>>> type(sampleTuple)
(class 'str')
>>> _
```

Looping through all values in a tuple

Looping through the values in a tuple is similar to looping through a list.

```
>>> a = (10, 20, 30)
>>> total1 = 0
>>> for i in range(len(a)):
        total1 += a[i]

>>> total1
```

```
60
>>> total2 = 0
>>> while (i < len(a)):
    total2 += a[i]
    i += 1

>>> total2
30
>>> total3 = 0
>>> for item in a:
    total3 += item

>>> total3
60
>>> for i in range(len(a)):
    if (i == 1):
        continue
    print(a[i])

10
30
>>> b = iter(a)
>>> for i in range(len(a)):
    print(next(b))

10
20
30
>>> _
```

Writing over a tuple

Writing over a tuple is tricky since it is not built to be overwritten. The prime advantage of tuples is that you can be assured that the values in it will be immutable.

Also, since the elements in the tuple, including the tuple object itself, cannot be changed (and these elements are all objects) they will contain less methods and attributes. Because of its simplistic and static nature and build, they are faster to process and loop into compared to the dynamic list.

And due to those reasons, tuples are often used to store large amounts of data with different types.

Generally, it is not recommended to create code to change tuples. You should have used lists instead if you are going to change its value and contents anyway.

Nonetheless, such situations arise like when the disadvantages of using lists outweighs the disadvantage of creating code to change the value and contents of a tuple.

Python does not allow changing a tuple's content. However, there are *workarounds*. One of them is to create a temporary list for your tuple's content.

You need to convert the tuple to a list using the list() function. Change the values you want in the list. And then assign the list as a tuple using the tuple() function. For example:

```
>>> sampleTuple = (1, 2, 3, 4, 5)
>>> sampleTuple
(1, 2, 3, 4, 5)
>>> temporaryList = list(sampleTuple)
>>> temporaryList
[1, 2, 3, 4, 5]
>>> temporaryList[0] = 999
>>> temporaryList
[999, 2, 3, 4, 5]
>>> sampleTuple = tuple(temporaryList)
>>> sampleTuple
(999, 2, 3, 4, 5)
>>> _
```

Dictionary

Dictionary is similar to lists, but instead of numerical indexes, it uses *keys*. Also, it uses curled brackets ({}) to enclose its items.

Keys are strings that are paired to values. You can access a value inside a dictionary by using its paired key. When assigning an item in a dictionary, you must input both key and value paired with a colon (:) in between them. E.g.

```
>>> sampleDictionary = {"name" : "admin", "password" : "pas123"}
>>> sampleDictionary["name"]
'admin'
>>> sampleDictionary["password"]
'pas123'
>>> sampleDictionary
{'name': 'admin', 'password': 'pas123'}
>>> _
```

Working with dictionaries

A dictionary is handy when you have data that have contextual values. It is also a nice alternative to using variables. You can just treat keys as variable names and values as the values of variables. For example:

```
>>> x = 1
>>> y = 2
>>> z = 3
>>> sampleDictionary = {"x": 1, "y": 2, "z": 3}
>>> _
```

Accessing values in a dictionary

As mentioned before, you can access a value in a dictionary by using the key of the value you want to access. Having a string key instead of a numerical index is a powerful advantage against list. Since you use a string, you can pair a key to a value with context.

Aside from that, you can still use numerical indices in dictionary. However, note that the dictionary will not automatically increment numerical keys or indices. Also, you are not restricted to start with 0. For example:

```
>>> sampleDictionary = {999: "sampleValue", "r": "randomValue", 0: "meh"}
>>> print(sampleDictionary["r"])
'randomValue'
>>> sampleDictionary[999]
'sampleValue'
>>> sampleDictionary[0]
'meh'
>>> _
```

Adding new Key-Value pairs

Unlike lists, you do not need to remember the current number of items that a dictionary holds to assign new items. You just need to make sure that the name of the key is unique compared to the ones already stored inside the dictionary.

For example:

```
>>> sampleDictionary["age"] = 9
>>> sampleDictionary["birthday"] = "January 1, 1980"
>>> sampleDictionary
{"age": 9, "birthday": "January 1, 1980"}
>>> _
```

Starting with an empty dictionary

You can start an empty dictionary by assigning a pair of curly brackets. For example:

```
>>> sampleDictionary = {}
>>> sampleDictionary
{}
>>> type(sampleDictionary)
<class 'dict'>
>>> _
```

Modifying values in a dictionary

Modifying values in a dictionary is as simple as assigning a new value to a key. For example:

```
>>> sampleDictionary["age"] = 9
>>> sampleDictionary["age"]
9
>>> sampleDictionary["age"] = 8
>>> sampleDictionary["age"]
8
>>> _
```

Removing key-Value pairs

You can remove a key and value pair by using the del function.

```
>>> sampleDictionary["key1"] = 135
>>> sampleDictionary["key2"] = 247
>>> sampleDictionary["key3"] = 358
>>> sampleDictionary
{'key1': 135, 'key2': 247, 'key3': 358}
>>> del sampleDictionary["key2"]
>>> sampleDictionary
{'key1': 135, 'key3': 358}
>>> _
```

Looping through a dictionary

You can loop a dictionary like a list, but it is a bit tricky because you need to get both keys and values. To pull this off, you need to use the "for" loop and the items() method of the dict class.

The items() method returns a dictionary's key and value pairs in the form of a tuple. Since it returns a tuple, the "for" loop statement can iterate on it and start a loop.

For example:

```
>>> sampleDictionary = {"a": 1, "b": 2, "c": 3}
>>> for key, value in sampleDictionary.items():
    print(key + " : " + str(value))

'a': 1
'b': 2
'c': 3
>>> _
```

Key and value are just variables. You can use any identifier or variables you want to receive data from the items() method. However, it is recommended that you use key and value for readability because both are conventionally used for this purpose.

Nesting

Aside from the usual strings and numbers, you can actually assign lists, tuples, and even dictionaries inside dictionaries, lists, and tuples.

For example:

```
>>> sampleList1 = [1, 2, 3, 4]
>>> sampleList2 = [5, 6, 7, sampleList1]
>>> sampleList2
[5, 6, 7, [1, 2, 3, 4]]
>>> sampleList2[0]
5
>>> sampleList2 [1]
6
>>> sampleList2 [2]
7
>>> sampleList2 [3]
[1, 2, 3, 4]
>>> sampleList2 [3][0]
1
```

```
>>> sampleList2 [3][1]
2
>>> sampleList2 [3][2]
3
>>> sampleList2 [3][3]
4
>>> sampleDictionary = {"a": 10, "b": 20, "ListItem": sampleList2}
>>> sampleDictionary
{'a': 10, 'b': 20, 'ListItem': [5, 6, 7, [1, 2, 3, 4]]}
>>> sampleDictionary["ListItem"]
[5, 6, 7, [1, 2, 3, 4]]
>>> sampleDictionary["ListItem"][3]
[1, 2, 3, 4]
>>> sampleDictionary["ListItem"][3][0]
1
>>> _
```

To access the values inside nested lists, tuples, and dictionaries, you just need to provide the keys and indices in proper succession. Here is an easier to read example using dictionaries:

```
>>> name = {"first": "John", "last": "Doe"}
>>> account = {"name": name}
>>> account
{'name': {'first': 'John', 'last': 'Doe'}}
>>> account["name"]["first"]
'John'
>>> account["name"]["last"]
'Doe'
>>> print(account["name"]["first"] + " " + account["name"]["last"])
John Doe
>>> _
```

Styling your code

Python has its own style guide under its Python Enhancement Proposals. It is written under PEP 008, and it was written by Guido van Rossum, Barry Warsaw, and Nick Coghlan. This section will summarize that document for easier reading.

Some of the styling proposals have been already mentioned in the early parts of this book. However, some of them will be mentioned again in the later parts of this book as reminders.

General Style Guide

- Do not update the style of already written code if it was already readable.

- Make sure that your code styling is consistent throughout a project.

- You can deviate from this styling guide if the recommendations will make your code unreadable.

- Imports should be done in separate statements. Importing will be discussed later in this book.

- Avoid placing unnecessary spaces before and after grouping symbols or delimiters.

- Avoid placing trailing whitespaces.

- Avoid the use of capital I, lowercase L, and capital O as single letter variables. They can easily confuse readers.

Indentation

- Use four spaces for each indentation level.

- If you are going to take advantage of Python's implicit line joining when using parentheses, use hanging indents.

- Align the indent with the opening delimiter (e.g., "(", "[", "{"). Or align the indent four spaces more than the first character of the parent line's position.

- Align the closing delimiter with first character of the parent line's position. Or you can align the closing delimiter with the opening delimiter.

```
>>> def sampleFunction():
    sampleList = [
        1, 2, 3, 4,
    ]

>>> _
```

Line length

- Limit the length for each line in Python by 79 characters.

- For flowing text or strings, limit the line by 72 characters.

- To improve readability, make the line joining explicit by adding a backslash character at the end of the line.

```
>>> sampleList = [
    "However, even if you can do this, do not.", \
```

```
        "You can encounter indentation errors doing things this way.", \
        "It does not mean that this \"\feature\" is useless.", \
        "Do this if the items take a lot of horizontal space." \
    ]

>>> _
```

Blank lines

- Surround class definitions and top-level functions with two blank lines while methods should be surrounded by one blank line. More about classes, methods, and functions later.

- You can separate statements from unrelated statements with a blank line. Remove all blank lines separating related statements.

Practice Exercise

1. Convert this table to a nested dictionary.

	First Name	**Last Name**	**Gender**	**Age**	**Position**	**Location**
Employee1	Johnny	Masaki	Male	25	Security	Cleveland Ohio
Employee2	George	Laurie	Male	25	Messenger	San Francisco, California
Employee3	Rowan	Bean	Female	67	Receptionist	London, UK
Employee4	Ford	Harrison	Male	53	Manager	New York, New York
Employee5	Roberta	Meyers	Female	36	Chief Financial Officer	Princeton, New Jersey

2. Display the contents of the above table by using a loop and the print() function.

Chapter Summary

Congratulations on your progress so far. Now, you already know the different types of data that you can use and process in Python. If you were able to perform the above practice exercises, then you have demonstrated a good understanding of the topic discussed. Therefore, you are now ready to proceed to the next chapter.

If you find yourself struggling to complete the practice exercise, don't worry. Just go through the topic again and have another go at the exercise. You'll get it.

The next chapter will prepare you to create complex and intelligent programs. In those lessons, you will be able to enhance the way you process the variables and literals you have into something more meaningful.

As long as you remember all the simple rules in using the variables and data types mentioned in this chapter, you can be confident that you can easily whip out a nice program.

Chapter 3: Solution

```python
firstName = [
  "Johnny", "George", "Rowan", "Ford", "Roberta"]
lastName = [
  "Masaki", "Laurie", "Bean", "Harrison", "Meyers"]
age = [
  25, 25, 67, 53, 36]
gender = [
  "Male", "Male", "Female", "Male", "Female"]
position = [
  "Security", "Messenger", "Receptionist", "Manager", "Chief Financial Officer"]
location = [
  "Cleveland, Ohio", "San Francisco, California", "London, UK", "New York, New York", "Princeton, New Jersey"]

employees = {}
for i in range(1, 6):
  employees["employee" + str(i)] = {
    "firstName": firstName[i - 1],
    "lastName": lastName[i - 1],
    "age": age[i - 1],
    "gender": gender[i - 1],
    "position": position[i - 1],
    "location": location[i - 1]
  }

for i in range(1, 6):
  x = "employee" + str(i)
  print(
    x + " : " +
    employees[x]["firstName"] + ", " +
    employees[x]["lastName"] + ", " +
    str(employees[x]["age"]) + ", " +
    employees[x]["gender"] + ", " +
    employees[x]["position"] + ", " +
    employees[x]["location"]
  )
```

> **Did you know?**

In the UK in 2015, it was *reported* that Python has overtaken French as the most popular language taught in primary schools, with 6 out of 10 parents preferring their children to learn it instead of French. Perhaps unsurprisingly, 75% of primary school children said they would rather learn how to program a robot than learn French.

Chapter 4

Conditions and Loops

Computing numbers and processing text are two basic functionalities that a computer program instructs a computer. An advanced or complex computer program has the capability to change its program flow. That is usually done by allowing it to make choices and decisions through conditional statements.

Condition statements are one of a few elements that control and direct your program's flow. Other common elements that can affect program flow are functions and loops.

A program with a neat and efficient program flow is like a create-your-own-adventure book. The progressions, outcomes, or results of your program depend on your user input and runtime environment.

For example, say that your computer program involves talking about cigarette consumption and vaping. You would not want minors to access the program to prevent any legal issues.

A simple way to prevent a minor from accessing your program is to ask the user his age. This information is then passed on to a common functionality within your program that decides if the age of the user is acceptable or not.

Programs and websites usually do this by asking for the user's birthday. That being said, the below example will only process the input age of the user for simplicity's sake.

```
>>> userAge = 12
>>> if (userAge < 18):
    print("You are not allowed to access this program.")
  else:
    print("You can access this program.")

You are not allowed to access this program.
>>> _
```

Here is the same code with the user's age set above 18.

```
>>> userAge = 19
>>> if (userAge < 18):
    print("You are not allowed to access this program.")
  else:
    print("You can access this program.")

You can access this program.
>>> _
```

The if and else operators are used to create condition statements. Condition statements have three parts. The conditional keyword, the Boolean value from a literal, variable, or expression, and the statements to execute.

In the above example, the keywords *if* and *else* were used to control the program's flow. The program checks if the variable **userAge** contains a value less than 18. If it does, a warning message is displayed. Otherwise, the program will display a welcome message.

The example used the comparison operator less than (<). It basically checks the values on either side of the operator symbol. If the value of the operand on the left side of the operator symbol was less than that on the right side, it will return True. Otherwise, if the value of the operand on the left side of the operator symbol was equal or greater than the value on the right side, it will return False.

"if" statements

The if keyword needs a literal, variable, or expression that returns a Boolean value, which can be True or False. Remember these two things:

1. If the value of the element next to the if keyword is equal to True, the program will process the statements within the if block.

2. If the value of the element next to the if keyword is equal to False, the program will skip or ignore the statements within the if block.

Else Statements

Else statements are used in conjunction with "if" statements. They are used to perform alternative statements if the preceding "if" statement returns False.

In the previous example, if the userAge is equal or greater than 18, the expression in the "if" statement will return False. And since the expression returns False on the "if" statement, the statements in the else statement will be executed.

On the other hand, if the userAge is less than 18, the expression in the "if" statement will return True. When that happens, the statements within the "if" statement will be executed while those in the else statement will be ignored.

Mind you, an else statement has to be preceded by an "if" statement. If there is none, the program will return an error. Also, you can put an else statement after another else statement as long as it precedes an "if" statement.

In summary:

1. If the "if" statement returns True, the program will skip the else statement that follows.

2. If the "if" statement returns False, the program will process the else statement code block.

Code Blocks

Earlier in this book, the definition of a code block was discussed. Just to jog your memory, code blocks are simply groups of statements or declarations that follow *if* and *else* statements.

Creating code blocks is an excellent way to manage your code and make it efficient. In the coming chapters, you will mostly be working with statements and scenarios that will keep you working on code blocks.

Aside from that, you will learn about variable scope as you progress. For now, you will mostly be creating code blocks "for" loops.

Loops

Loops are an essential part of programming. Every program that you use and see use loops.

Loops are blocks of statements that are executed repeatedly until a condition is met. It also starts when a condition is satisfied.

By the way, did you know that your monitor refreshes the image itself 60 times a second? Refresh means displaying a new image. The computer itself has a looping program that creates a new image on screen.

You may not create a program with a complex loop to handle the display, but you will definitely use one in one of your programs. A good example is a small snippet of program that requires the user to login using a password.

For example:

```
>>> password = "secret"
>>> userInput = ""
>>> while (userInput != password):
    userInput = input()
```

This example will ask for a user input. On the text cursor, you need to type the password and then press the Enter key. The program will keep on asking for a user input until you type the word secret.

While

Loops are easy to code. All you need is the correct keyword, a conditional value, and statements you want to execute repeatedly.

One of the keywords that you can use to loop is *while*. While is like an "if" statement. If its condition is met or returns True, it will start the loop. Once the program executes the last statement in the code block, it will recheck the while statement and condition again. If the condition still returns True, the code block will be executed again. If the condition returns False, the code block will be ignored, and the program will execute the next line of code. For example

```
>>> i = 1
>>> while i < 6:
    print(i)
    i += 1
1
2
3
4
5
>>> _
```

For Loop

While the *while* loop statement loops until the condition returns false, the "for" loop statement will loop at a set number of times depending on a string, tuple, or list. For example:

```
>>> carBrands = ["Toyota", "Volvo", "Mitsubishi", "Volkswagen"]
>>> for brands in carBrands:
    print(brands)

Toyota
Volvo
Mitsubishi
Volkswagen
>>> _
```

Break

Break is a keyword that stops a loop. Here is one of the previous examples combined with break.

For example:

```
>>> password = "secret"
>>> userInput = ""
>>> while (userInput != password):
```

```
    userInput = input()
    break
    print("This will not get printed.")

Wrongpassword
>>> _
```

As you can see here, the while loop did not execute the print keyword and did not loop again after an input was provided since the break keyword came after the input assignment.

The break keyword allows you to have better control of your loops. For example, if you want to loop a code block in a set amount of times without using sequences, you can use while and break.

```
>>> x = 0
>>> while (True):
    x += 1
    print(x)
    if (x == 5):
        break

1
2
3
4
5
>>> _
```

Using a counter, variable x (any variable will do of course) with an integer that increments every loop in this case, condition and break is common practice in programming. In most programming languages, counters are even integrated in loop statements. Here is a "for" loop with a counter in JavaScript.

```
for(i = 0; i < 10; i++) {

    alert(i);

}
```

This script will loop for ten times. On one line, the counter variable is declared, assigned an initial value, a conditional expression was set, and the increments for the counter are already coded.

Infinite Loop

You should always be aware of the greatest problem with coding loops: infinity loops. Infinity loops are loops that never stop. And since they never stop, they can easily make your program become unresponsive, crash, or hog all your computer's resources. Here is an example similar with the previous one but without the counter and the usage of break.

```
>>> while (True):
    print("This will never end until you close the program")

This will never end until you close the program
This will never end until you close the program
This will never end until you close the program
```

Whenever possible, always include a counter and break statement in your loops. Doing this will prevent your program from having infinite loops.

Continue

The continue keyword is like a soft version of break. Instead of breaking out from the whole loop, "continue" just breaks away from one loop and directly goes back to the loop statement. For example:

```
>>> password = "secret"
>>> userInput = ""
>>> while (userInput != password):
    userInput = input()
    continue
    print("This will not get printed.")

Wrongpassword
Test
secret
>>> _
```

When this example was used on the break keyword, the program only asks for user input once regardless of anything you enter and it ends the loop if you enter anything. This version, on the other hand, will still persist on asking input until you put the right password. However, it will always skip on the print statement and always go back directly to the while statement.

Here is a practical application to make it easier to know the purpose of the continue statement.

```
>>> carBrands = ["Toyota", "Volvo", "Mitsubishi", "Volkswagen"]
>>> for brands in carBrands:
    if (brands == "Volvo"):
        continue
    print("I have a " + brands)

I have a Toyota
I have a Mitsubishi
I have a Volkswagen
>>> _
```

When you are parsing or looping a sequence, there are items that you do not want to process. You can skip the ones you do not want to process by using a continue statement. In the above example, the program did not print "I have a Volvo", because it hit **continue** when a Volvo was selected. This caused it to go back and process the next car brand in the list.

Error Handling

Sometimes, errors happen during the program. This might be caused by a bad code or bad user input. Most of the time, it is the former.

Python immediately ends a program whenever errors are encountered. However, what if you want the show to continue despite these errors?

You might want to know what happens with the other code you have written after the line that produced the error. You want to know if they are also problematic. That is when error handling is useful.

Error handling is a programming process wherein you assume control of the program's errors from Python. Instead of just letting Python close your program, performing error handling can let you run code and continue with the program if an error is encountered.

Try and Except

One of the ways to handle errors is to use the keywords *try* and *except*. Try is like if. However, instead of testing a literal, variable, or expression's truth value, try only tests if the code block under it will generate an error.

"Except" statements works together with "try" statements. The purpose of except is to execute a code block when the code within the try statement returns an error. If you omit except and only use try, you will get an error. For example:

```
>>> try:
    a = 1
```

```
    b = "a"
    c = a + b
except:
    print("There is an error on the try code block.")

There is an error on the try code block.
>>> _
```

In the above example, the try code block "tried" to add an integer and a string. Using the (+) operator like that will confuse Python. After all, the behavior of the (+) operator depends on the data type you use with it. If you use numbers, it will act as an addition operator. If you use strings, it will act as a concatenate operator.

Normally, without the try statement, this will happen if you add an integer and a string:

```
>>> a = 1
>>> b = "a"
>>> c = a + b
Traceback (most recent call last):
  File "<stdin>", line 1, in <module>
TypeError: unsupported operand type(s) for +: 'int' and 'str'
>>> _
```

Anyway, note that despite the fact the previous example's try block had an error, the print statement in the "except" code block got executed. That's the essence of using try and except statements for error handling. Nonetheless, there are precise ways to use these keywords and these involve specifying the code that will be run depending on the error that was caught by the program.

We will discuss more about try and except statements in the later parts of this book. In there, you will learn how to effectively manage exceptions and error. More importantly, you will learn how to control the program whenever it encounters an error.

Variable Styling

Here are a few quick reminders from Python's style guide (PEP 8).

- As much as possible, sparingly use global variables. And when you truly need one, just make sure that the set of global variables you will use is for a single module only.

- Again, do not use the lower case l, uppercase O or the uppercase I for single letter variables. As you can see right now, it is difficult to differentiate l, I, and 1 and O and 0 from each other.

Practice Exercise

For this chapter, create a choose-your-adventure program. The program should provide users with two options. It must also have at least five choices and have at least two different endings.

You must also use dictionaries to create dialogues.

Here is an example:

```
creepometer = 1
prompt = "\nType 1 or 2 then press enter...\n\n ::> "
clearScreen = ("\n" * 25)
scenario = [
    "You see your crush at the other side of the road on your way to school.",
    "You notice that her handkerchief fell on the ground.",
    "You heard a ring. She reached on to her pocket to get her phone and stopped.",
    "Both of you reached the pedestrian crossing, but its currently red light.",
    "You got her attention now and you instinctively grabbed your phone."
]

choice1 = [
    "Follow her using your eyes and cross when you reach the intersection.",
    "Pick it up and give it to her.",
    "Walk pass her.",
    "Smile and wave at her.",
    "Ask for her number."
]

choice2 = [
    "Cross the road and jaywalk, so you will be behind her.",
    "Pick it up and keep it for yourself.",
    "Stop and pretend you are tying your shoes.",
    "Tap her shoulders.",
    "Take a picture of her using your phone."
]

result1 = [
    "A car honked at you and she noticed you. She walked a bit faster.",
    "You called her and you gave her the handkerchief.",
    "She noticed you as you walked pass her, but she focused on the call she got.",
    "She smiled and waved back.",
    "She started to think about it."
```

```
]

result2 = [
    "You walked casually and crossed the pedestrian lane.",
    "You stashed away her handkerchief on your pocket.",
    "She noticed you and her rightbrow rose.",
    "She turned towards you.",
    "Her eyes suddenly become bloodshot red."
]

ending1 = [
    "She grabbed her phone, and typed some numbers.",
    "You became giddy.",
    "After a second, she showed you her phone.",
    "Her number was on the screen.",
    "You quickly fiddled with your phone and typed in her digits.",
    "She walked away towards the school gate."
]

ending2 = [
    "She politely turned down your request.",
    "She walked away towards the school gate.",
    "She looked back at you for a moment.",
    "Your eyes met for a moment.",
    "Then she turned away.",
    "There is hope for you, you thought."
]

ending3 = [
    "Her right hand moved and the next thing you saw was the sky.",
    "Your life flashed in front of you.",
    "Her scream brought you back to reality.",
    "Your left cheek was scorched hot as the pain radiate from it.",
    "You then asked yourself why.",
    "That was the last time you saw her."
]

instructions = [
    "Here are the instructions on how to play this game.",
    "1. To play and complete this game, you must enter your choices when asked.",
    "2. Press enter to proceed with the next dialog.",
    "3. The choices you make changes the ending of the game.",
```

```
    "Press enter whenever you are ready."
]

print(clearScreen)

for i in range(len(instructions)):
    print(instructions[i])

input()

print(clearScreen)

for i in range(len(scenario)):

    input(scenario[i])
    print("1. " + choice1[i])
    print("2. " + choice2[i])
    answer = ""

    while (True):
        answer = input(prompt)
        if(answer == "1" or answer == "2"):
            break

    print("\n")
    if(answer == "1"):
        input(result1[i])
        creepometer -= 1
    else:
        input(result2[i])
        creepometer += 1

if(creepometer < 0):
    for i in range(len(ending1)):
        input(ending1[i])

if(creepometer == 0):
    for i in range(len(ending2)):
        input(ending2[i])

if(creepometer > 0):
    for i in range(len(ending3)):
```

```
    input(ending3[i])

input("Thank you for playing the game!")
```

By the way, the clearScreen variable contains multiplied \n (new line) characters. Printing numerous new lines can push the previous lines upwards, which basically clears the screen.

You can make the input() function add a prompt by passing a string inside its parentheses. Also, it is an excellent way to "pause" the program and wait for users to press enter to continue.

Have fun!

Chapter Summary

By just learning loops and conditional statements, your programming prowess becomes robust! The excitement starts at this point. You're making great progress. Keep it up!

With loops and conditions, you can start to do almost anything. They also give you better understanding with regards to how programming works. As you can see in the practice exercise, it is definitely proof that you can already do something worthwhile at your current level.

Speaking of choose-your-adventure programs, some popular text-based games are done like the example. If you are interested in developing games, this is the start. Show your text based adventure to your friends.

With try and except statements, you can be confident handling errors and exceptions. You can use these statements to create band aid solutions while you explore and create the rest of your program. Note that try and except statements will be further explored at the end of this book.

For now, the next step towards your goal of becoming a rock star Python programmer is learning about functions and modules. Let's get to it!

Chapter 4: Solution

```
creepometer = 1
prompt = "\nType 1 or 2 then press enter...\n\n ::> "
clearScreen = ("\n" * 25)
scenario = [
    "You see your crush at the other side of the road on your way to school.",
    "You notice that her handkerchief fell on the ground.",
    "You heard a ring. She reached on to her pocket to get her phone and stopped.",
    "Both of you reached the pedestrian crossing, but its currently red light.",
    "You got her attention now and you instinctively grabbed your phone."
]

choice1 = [
    "Follow her using your eyes and cross when you reach the intersection.",
    "Pick it up and give it to her.",
    "Walk pass her.",
    "Smile and wave at her.",
    "Ask for her number."
]

choice2 = [
    "Cross the road and jaywalk, so you will be behind her.",
    "Pick it up and keep it for yourself.",
    "Stop and pretend you are tying your shoes.",
    "Tap her shoulders.",
    "Take a picture of her using your phone."
]

result1 = [
    "A car honked at you and she noticed you. She walked a bit faster.",
    "You called her and you gave her the handkerchief.",
    "She noticed you as you walked pass her, but she focused on the call she got.",
    "She smiled and waved back.",
    "She started to think about it."
]

result2 = [
    "You walked casually and crossed the pedestrian lane.",
    "You stashed away her handkerchief on your pocket.",
    "She noticed you and her rightbrow rose.",
    "She turned towards you.",
```

```
    "Her eyes suddenly become bloodshot red."
]

ending1 = [
    "She grabbed her phone, and typed some numbers.",
    "You became giddy.",
    "After a second, she showed you her phone.",
    "Her number was on the screen.",
    "You quickly fiddled with your phone and typed in her digits.",
    "She walked away towards the school gate."
]

ending2 = [
    "She politely turned down your request.",
    "She walked away towards the school gate.",
    "She looked back at you for a moment.",
    "Your eyes met for a moment.",
    "Then she turned away.",
    "There is hope for you, you thought."
]

ending3 = [
    "Her right hand moved and the next thing you saw was the sky.",
    "Your life flashed in front of you.",
    "Her scream brought you back to reality.",
    "Your left cheek was scorched hot as the pain radiate from it.",
    "You then asked yourself why.",
    "That was the last time you saw her."
]

instructions = [
    "Here are the instructions on how to play this game.",
    "1. To play and complete this game, you must enter your choices when asked.",
    "2. Press enter to proceed with the next dialog.",
    "3. The choices you make changes the ending of the game.",
    "Press enter whenever you are ready."
]

print(clearScreen)

for i in range(len(instructions)):
    print(instructions[i])
```

```
input()

print(clearScreen)

for i in range(len(scenario)):

    input(scenario[i])
    print("1. " + choice1[i])
    print("2. " + choice2[i])
    answer = ""

    while (True):
        answer = input(prompt)
        if(answer == "1" or answer == "2"):
            break

    print("\n")
    if(answer == "1"):
        input(result1[i])
        creepometer -= 1
    else:
        input(result2[i])
        creepometer += 1

if(creepometer < 0):
    for i in range(len(ending1)):
        input(ending1[i])

if(creepometer == 0):
    for i in range(len(ending2)):
        input(ending2[i])

if(creepometer > 0):
    for i in range(len(ending3)):
        input(ending3[i])

input("Thank you for playing the game!")
```

Did you know?

The first computer programmer was a female, named Ada Lovelace

Chapter 5

Functions and Modules

Functions are code blocks that are given an identifier. This identifier can be used to call the function. Calling a function makes the program execute the function regardless of where it is located within the code.

To create a function, you need to use the "def" keyword. Def basically defines, and when you use it to create a function, you can call it as defining a function. For example:

```
>>> def doSomething():
    print("Hello functioning world!")

>>> doSomething()
Hello functioning world!
>>> _
```

Creating and calling a function is easy. The primary purpose of a function is to allow you to organize, simplify, and modularize your code. Whenever you have a set of code that you will need to execute in sequence from time to time, defining a function for that set of code will save you time and space in your program. Instead of repeatedly typing code or even copy pasting, you simply define a function.

Arguments and Parameters

Aside from serving as a quick way to execute a block of code, functions can accept arguments through its parameters. What are arguments and parameters anyway? Before I offer any explain, look at the below example:

```
>>> def saySomething(thisIsaParameter):
    print(thisIsaParameter)

>>> saySomething("This Is An Argument")
This Is An Argument
>>> _
```

Think of it this way: parameters are questions and arguments are answers. The keyword print has the parameter that requires you to input a string as an argument. Whenever you use the keyword print, it is asking you, "What do you want me to print?" You then reply with the string that you want the print keyword to display on the screen.

In technical terms, parameters are private variables of functions. Whenever you call a function and indicate an argument for the parameter, you are basically assigning a value to the parameter, which the function can use as a regular variable.

Note the word *private*. Since parameters are functions' private variables, no other function(s) can use them. Also, variables declared and used for the first time in a function will also be unavailable to others.

Outside the scope of a function, all of its parameters and private variables are erased. This means that you cannot access their assigned value once the function has *completed* execution. For example:

```
>>> def sampFunc(x):
    print(x)

>>> sampFunc("Sample String")
Sample String
>>> x
Traceback (most recent call last):
  File "<stdin>", line 1, in <module>
NameError: name 'x' is not defined
>>> _
```

By the way, the parentheses are important. They separate your parameters and arguments from your function's identifier or name. When calling a function, you always need to place those parentheses even if you have not set a parameter.

More about private variables and related topics will be discussed later.

Parameters Require Arguments

You cannot call a function with parameters without an argument. If you do, you will receive an error. For example:

```
>>> def sampFunc(x):
    print(x)

>>> sampFunc()
Traceback (most recent call last):
  File "<stdin>", line 1, in <module>
TypeError: y() missing 1 required positional argument: 'x'
>>> _
```

Multiple Parameters

You can assign two or more parameters in a function. For example:

```
>>> def simpOp(x, y):
    z = x + y
    print(z)

>>> simpOp(1, 2)
3
>>> _
```

Passing Arguments By Value, Reference, and Assignment

In most programming languages, passing an argument using variables to a parameter can be done in two ways: value and reference.

If you pass an argument by value, the function will only take the value of the variable and assign it to the parameter. Here is an example using Visual Basic 6:

Function f(ByVal a as Integer, ByVal b as Integer)

a = a + b

End Function

Sub main()

x = 1

y = 2

Call f(x + y)

End Sub

Variables x and y will still hold the value 1 and 2 respectively after calling the function f.

If you pass an argument by reference, the function will assign the parameter the variable itself. Any changes or manipulation on the parameter will reflect on the variable assigned.

Here is an example using Visual Basic 6:

Function f(ByRef a as Integer, ByRef b as Integer)

a = a + b

End Function

Sub main()

   x = 1

   y = 2

   Call f(x + y)

End Sub

Variable y will still hold the value 2 while variable x will have the value 3 after calling the function f.

Python works differently. Instead of passing variables as values and references, they are passed by assignment.

It means that Python will pass the variable by value or reference depending on the type of data the variable contains. For example:

```
>>> x = 10
>>> def increment(y):
    y += 1

>>> increment(x)
>>> x
10
>>> _
```

Python will pass by value if the variable contains an immutable object like a string. Python will pass by reference if the variable contains a mutable object like a list.

```
>>> x = [1, 2, 3, 4]
>>> def addItem(y):
    y += [5, 6, 7, 8]

>>> addItem(x)
>>> x
[1, 2, 3, 4, 5, 6, 7, 8]
>>> _
```

Passing by reference seems convenient, especially if you need to manipulate data in a variable fast. However, if you have strings and numbers, you are stuck with passing by value. For example:

```
>>> x = 10
>>> y = 3
```

```
>>> def exponent(a, b):
    a = a**b
    print(a)

>>> exponent(x, y)
1000
>>>
```

However, you want the value to be assigned to x instead of just printing it. You might try to solve this kind of problem by assigning the value to variable x directly inside the function like this:

```
>>> x = 10
>>> y = 3
>>> def exponent(a, b):
    x = a**b
    print(x)

>>> exponent(x, y)
1000
>>> x
10
>>>
```

Unfortunately, that will not work since Python will treat the variable x inside the function as one of the function's *private* variable. Despite having the same name as the variable x outside the scope of the function, the variable x inside the function is different from it.

One way to mitigate this kind of problem is to use the keyword **global**. Note that variables outside the scope of functions are considered global variables. However, Global variables can be used inside functions, but you need to tell Python that it is a global variable by using the keyword **global**. Here is an example:

```
>>> x = 10
>>> y = 3
>>> def exponent(a, b):
    global x
    x = a**b
    print(x)

>>> exponent(x, y)
1000
>>> x
1000
```

```
>>> _
```

It seems that it solved the problem of not having a pass by reference for numbers. However, this is bad coding. Yes, you can do it, but it does not always mean that if you can do something, it is good.

First of all, most developers discourage the use of global variable. This is a debatable topic.

Second, this way of assigning value to a variable from a function is weak. What if you have a different variable and want to do the same to it. This piece of code will not do since it only changes variable x. It is true there is a workaround by making x as a temporary variable to hold the value of the function. For example:

```
>>> x = 10
>>> y = 3
>>> z = 0
>>> def exponent(a, b):
    global z
    z = a**b
    print(z)

>>> exponent(x, y)
1000
>>> x
10
>>> z
1000
>>> x = z
>>> x
1000
>>> _
```

It works, but you are still using a global variable and it makes your code messy. Yes, that is messy by default standards.

The third reason why the previous example is a bad/inefficient code is that there is a better way to do it. And that is by using the *return* keyword.

Returning Value

The return keyword makes a function return a value. For example:

```
>>> def concat(string1, string2):
    return string1 + string2
```

```
>>> x = concat("Text1", "Text2")
>>> x
'Text1Text2'
>>> _
```

A function can return a value even if it does not have parameters. For example:

```
>>> def piString():
    return "3.14159265359"
>>> x = piString()
>>> x
'3.14159265359'
>>> _
```

As you can see, using the keyword method makes it simpler for you to retrieve a value from a function without relying on global variables. Return allows you to create clean and efficient code.

Mutable and Immutable Objects

Now that you know the return statement, you can now work on passing arguments by reference and by value without worrying about the variable's mutability. By the way, mutability is a characteristic of an object that refers to its ability to mutate. Whenever you process and *change* data, you mutate it.

Immutable objects are integers, float, Boolean, string, and tuples. You can easily understand why tuples are immutable because they are lists that cannot be changed. However, you might get confused why numbers, strings, and Boolean values are immutable. After all, you can change or reassign the number assigned to variable x anytime.

The keywords there are change and reassign. For example:

```
>>> x = 1
>>> x
1
>>> x = 2
>>> x
2
>>> _
```

Remember that everything in Python is an object. This includes numbers, strings, Boolean values, and etcetera. In the above example, 1 and 2 are two separate objects. Instead of mutating the object 1 assigned to variable x, you just *replace* it with object 2.

Here is another example:

```
>>> x = 1
>>> x
1
>>> x += 5
>>> x
6
>>> _
```

Python thinks of this as adding object 1 and object 5, and change the value of variable x to object 6. The only thing that changes here is the *value* of variable x. The objects 1, 5, and 6 did not change. They were just replaced.

Now, it is time for mutable objects. A list is a good example of a mutable object. Here is an example:

```
>>> a = ["a", "b", "c"]
>>> a
['a', 'b', 'c']
>>> a.extend(['d', 'e'])
>>> a
['a', 'b', 'c', 'd', 'e']
>>> _
```

In here, instead of just reassigning a value, the list was extended. The extended list is still the same object list. Therefore, it mutated to something bigger instead of being replaced completely.

To make mutability of objects much easier, it will be best to use the *id* keyword.

```
>>> id(1)
1730951424
>>> id(2)
1730951440
>>> x = 1
>>> id(x)
1730951424
>>> x = 2
>>> id(x)
1730951440
```

As you can see, the ids of objects 1 and 2 are different. And when you assign object 1 and 2 to the variable x, its id becomes the same with the object that is assigned.

Now, do this experiment with lists.

```
>>> list1 = [1, 2, 3]
>>> id(list1)
3491240
>>> list2 = [1, 2, 3, 4]
>>> id(list2)
3492400
>>> x = list1
>>> id(x)
3491240
>>> x.extend([4])
>>> x
[1, 2, 3, 4]
>>> id(x)
3491240
>>> _
```

As you can see, the id of the list [1, 2, 3] and the id of the list [1, 2, 3, 4] are different. However, the list [1, 2, 3] did not change when we extended it by adding [4] to make it similar to the list [1, 2, 3, 4]. What happened was the list was not replaced, but was mutated instead.

Passing List by Value

You can use a function for passing list by value by simply using slice. For example:

```
>>> tempList = [1, 2, 3, 4]
>>> def function(mutable):
    mutable += [5, 6, 7, 8]
    print(mutable)

>>> function(tempList[:])
[1, 2, 3, 4, 5, 6, 7, 8]
>>> tempList
[1, 2, 3, 4]
>>> _
```

Anonymous Functions or Lambda

Using an anonymous function is a convenient way to write one-line functions that require arguments and return a value. It uses the keyword lambda. Despite having a purpose of being a one liner, it can have numerous parameters. For example:

```
>>> average = lambda x, y, z: (x + y + z) / 3
>>> x = average(10, 20, 30)
>>> x
20.0
>>> average(12, 51, 231)
98.0
>>> _
```

Variable Scopes

Since global and private variables have been mentioned, this section will discuss variable scopes.

There are two types of variables: global and local.

Global variables are available throughout the program. When using them inside functions, you use the keyword global. In some programming languages, global variables are referred to as public variables.

Local variables are only available inside a code block where it is used. The previous sections referred to it as private variables for simplification purposes. Local variables can be used by the function that declared or used it and are deleted once the function ends.

For accuracy's sake, this book will now refer to global variables as global variables and local variables as local variables. Public and private variables can easily have a different connotation. And this can be confusing once you start dealing with modules.

Optional Arguments and Default Values

At this point, we know that functions require arguments to be passed to parameters. However, there are cases where you do not have an argument to pass or your arguments' values rarely deviate. In those cases, you need to use optional arguments and default values. For example:

```
>>> def addOrMultiply(number1, number2, operation = "add"):
    if (operation == "add"):
        print(number1 + number2)
    if (operation == "multiply"):
        print(number1 * number2)
```

```
>>> addOrMultiply(12, 51)
63
>>> addOrMultiply(12, 51, "add")
63
>>> addOrMultiply(12, 51, "multiply")
612
>>> addOrMultiply(12, 51, "asld jkhb")
>>> _
```

Arbitrary Arguments

If you want to pass an unknown number of arguments to your function, it can be difficult to prepare parameters for them. For example, what if you want to process the names of the students who attended a certain class? The names can easily vary from one to the maximum number of students who can attend class.

For that kind of scenarios, you can format your function like this:

```
>>> def classNames(*args):
        for i in range(len(args)):
            print(args[i])

>>> classNames("John", "William", "Joe")
John
William
Joe
>>> _
```

Note that *args* indicates that the function will accept arbitrary number of arguments. All of the arguments will be sent as items inside a tuple variable named args. When looping through the tuple args using for, you can use a variable to contain the current item being parsed inside the tuple. With that in mind, the previous example can be written as:

```
>>> def classNames(*args):
        for arg in args:
            print(arg)

>>> classNames("John", "William", "Joe")
John
William
Joe
>>> _
```

You can include regular parameters inside a function that uses *args. However, note that you should place *args as the last parameter. For example:

```
>>> def classNames(teachername, *args):
        print("Teacher: " + teachername)
        for i in range(len(args)):
            print("Student " + str(i + 1) + ": " + args[i])

>>> classNames("Winchester", "John", "William", "Joe")
Teacher: Winchester
Student 1: John
Student 2: William
Student 3: Joe
>>> _
```

Also, *args are used to allow the function to accept "non-keyworded" list that will result to a tuple. You use **kwargs, on the other hand, to allow the function to accept "keyworded" list that will result to a dictionary.

Storing Functions in Modules

Writing a huge program in one file can be cumbersome. A regular program like calculator can have hundreds of functions, and each of those functions can contain five to nine statements. If one statement equals one line of code, writing a small program with a hundred functions can make you deal with 500 to 900 lines of codes.

Even if Python is one of many programming languages revered due to its syntax' simplicity and code readability, having to find, write, and edit code in the midst of 900 lines can be tedious and confusing. When you exceed roughly 100 lines of codes or at least 10 functions, then it makes sense to use modules.

What is a module anyway?

A module is simply a Python (.py) file that consists of python code. In programming, the common hierarchy is this:

Program > Modules > Functions > Statements > Variables/Expressions/Data

A program contains modules. A module contains functions. A function contains statements. A statement contains variables, expressions, data, and data. Depending on the complexity of your program, that hierarchy can easily change.

The question now is, "How to create a module?" Creating a module in Python is simple. You just need to write or paste all the functions and statements you want to be contained, and save it as a *.py file. That is it. You have a new module.

Note that a module can use other modules. To use a module, you need to import them in the program using the *import* keyword.

For example, here is a function inside your module. And this module will be saved as sample.py.

```
def sampleFunction():
    print("Hello World")
def sampleFunction2():
    print("Hello Again")
```
Here is how to use the sampleFunction function from the sample.py module.
```
>>> import sample
>>> sample.sampleFunction()
Hello World
>>> _
```

Note that the module must be in the same directory as the program/main module (or the one importing it) for the module to be imported. If not, you will get an error message.

```
>>> import nonExistingModule
Traceback (most recent call last):
  File "<stdin>", line 1, in <module>
ModuleNotFoundError: No module named 'nonExistingModule'
>>> _
```

When you use the import keyword, you will have access to all the functions inside a module. Importing a module this way will make Python treat the functions in the module as methods of the module object. In simpler terms, you will need to mention the object and use the accessor operator (.) to call the function.

If you want to use only one or a specific number of functions from the module and integrate them in the current module as if they are defined in it, you can use the *from* keyword together with import. For example:

```
>>> from sample import sampleFunction
>>> sampleFunction()
Hello World
>>> _
```
You can import multiple functions by doing this:
```
>>> from sample import sampleFunction, sampleFunction2
>>> sampleFunction2()
Hello Again
>>> _
```
If you want to use the "from" keyword to get all the function from a module, you can use the asterisk or wildcard operator (*).

```
>>> from sample import *
>>> sampleFunction()
```

```
Hello World
>>> _
```

Note that you will get an error if you try to call a function without the module object and accessor if you only use import.

```
>>> import sample
>>> sampleFunction()
Traceback (most recent call last):
  File "<stdin>", line 1, in <module>
NameError: name 'sampleFunction' is not defined
>>> _
```

Function and Module Styles

This section will just provide you with reminders from PEP8.

- Function names should always be in lowercase and you should separate multiple words in a function with underscores.

- Remember that the styling tips and naming methods for function is the same with the ones for variables.

- Always follow the prevailing style in the code. If the code already follows mixed case convention, adapt to it instead of trying to change everything,

- Always prevent using a function name similar to a keyword. Python is a dynamic language, and you can easily use keywords as identifiers. Use synonyms if possible.

- Add a trailing underscore if a function's name is the same with a keyword and you cannot think of an appropriate replacement. Do not corrupt the spelling. For example, use the name class_ instead of cls.

- Module names should always be in lowercase. Use underscores if they can improve readability and truly needed. The same goes with Python packages.

Practice Exercises

This time, improve this basic calculator program by adding functions you can find in a scientific calculator. This chapter discussed importing modules, which is required to have access to Mathematical functions like factorial(), cos(), sin(), etcetera.

Since the math module was not covered, just do away with the following features of a scientific calculator:

- C

- MC, MR, MS, M+, M-

- ±

- 1/x

- 10^x, x^y, x^2, x^3

- Π

- Mod

Chapter Summary

Functions give you great control in your program. Instead of writing statements in a series, you can just create function code blocks and call them when you need the statements within them to be executed.

It also allows you to create cleaner and more organized code. You will not need to copy paste code again and again. Also, your code will be more readable.

On the other hand, modules can make your life easier. You can store your big chunks of code in one file and focus on the one you are currently coding. In addition, you will not need to go through a tedious process whenever you want to edit a part in your program. Just remember the module where you saved the code you want to edit, and just open it.

Aside from those, using modules opens a variety of opportunities to you as a programmer. If you are in a hurry to create a program, just look for modules that will suit your needs. Also, you can now access some of Python's library modules, which can add more functionality to your programs.

In addition, modules will allow you to reuse code from project to project. Say that you already made a specific function that you commonly use in all of your projects. Just save it in a module, and import them in the project you are working on.

Modules make you an efficient and smart programmer.

Now that we've covered functions and modules, you should now move on to object oriented programming. You can consider the following chapters advanced and can be somewhat optional for a beginner.

However, if you're feeling up to it and want to further improve your skills in Python and programming in general, join me in the next chapters.

Chapter 5: Solution

```
def mc():
    memory = 0
def mr():
    current = memory
def ms():
    memory = current
def mplus():
    current += memory
def mminus():
    current -= memory
def plusminus():
    current *= -1
def c():
    current = 0
def mod():
    current =  a % b
def pi():
    current = 3.14159265359
def reciprocal():
    current = 1/current
def exponent():
    current = a**b
def square():
    current = a**2
def cube():
    current = a**3
```

Did you know?

The first high-level (very close to real English that we use to communicate) programming language was FORTRAN, invented in 1954 by IBM's John Backus

Chapter 6

Object Oriented Programming (OOP)

What is Object Oriented Programming?

Object Oriented Programming (OOP) is a programming technique, method, or paradigm. To understand this concept easier, you must know about imperative, structured, and procedural programming.

Imperative

In the earlier sections of this book, you have been shown imperative programming. You only use statements to create and manipulate data. The program starts with the first line of code and ends with the last line.

Every beginner starts with imperative. This paradigm is the best way to introduce programming to people. Imperative programing is also easier to read and digest. However, it easily loses its readability when the lines of codes increase by the hundreds.

Structured

Dealing with conditional statements, loops, and code blocks transitioned you to structural or structured programming. You learn to group statements into blocks that aim to perform a single goal and introduce logical branches in your program through controlling the flow of the program using conditional and loop statements.

Procedural

When you learned about functions, you were introduced to procedural programming. Procedural programming is a subset of imperative programming combined with structured programming.

At this point, you group your assignment, conditional, and loop statements in functions. You also group your functions into modules, which allows you to take advantage of modular programming.

You use functions to repeatedly and conditionally perform series of statements to achieve certain goals in your program.

Object Oriented

If you recall, I mentioned earlier that every element in Python is an object. A number is an object. A list is an object. And even a function is an object. However, using objects does not automatically make you a programmer that performs OOP.

In object oriented programming, you perform imperative, structured, and procedural. The biggest exception is the usage of classes and objects.

What exactly are classes and objects anyway?

Objects are elements in a program that contains attributes, properties, and methods. Attributes are actually variables of an object and methods are functions of an object. Properties, on the other hand, are attributes with programmer defined setter, getter, and delete methods.

Creating properties will not be discussed in this book.

Classes, on the other hand, are an object's template. When you define a class, you code the attributes and methods of any object that is created using the class as its template.

For example:

```
>>> x = [1, 2, 3, 4]
>>> id(x)
4408744
>>> x.extend([5])
>>> x
[1, 2, 3, 4, 5]
>>> _
```

In this example, [1, 2, 3, 4] is an attribute of the object 4408744. It is a variable with a value that can be obtained and assigned with another value. Extend, on the other hand, is a method that do certain tasks in the object. And list is object 4408744's class.

Creating and Using a Class

To create a class in Python, you need to use the *class* keyword. Creating classes is similar to creating a function. Here is a simple example:

```
>>> class student:
    def __init__(self, name, gender, age, sid):
        self.name = name
        self.gender = gender
        self.age = age
        self.sid = sid
    def details(self):
        print("Name: " + self.name)
        print("ID: " + self.sid)
        print("Age: " + self.age)
        print("Gender: " + self.gender)

>>> _
```

The example created a class named student. The code has done three things: create attributes, defined a method, and set the initial parameters.

The attributes created were name, gender, age, and sid. The method created was details().

By the way, the __init__ or initializer function is a special function that gets executed when you create an object from a class for the first time. All objects in Python have this method. Furthermore, note you have *two* underscore before and after init.

Making an Instance from a Class and Instantiating a Child Object

The next example will show how to create a method using the student class.

```
>>> student1 = student("Johnny", "Male", "18", "1000121")
>>> student1.details()
Name: Johnny
ID: 1000121
Age: 18
Gender: Male
>>> _
```

The example created an object by using the class name and providing arguments to the parameters listed in the initializer method. By the way, the "self" identifier is not a keyword. It is a convention that you can use to refer to the object or the object that called the method. More about this will be explained later.

In the case of the init method, the self refers to the object itself. Also, since the value of self is already established as the object, you do not need to give it an argument. Just proceed with the other parameters.

Objects created from a class are called *instances*.

Working With Classes and Instances

Classes and instances are handy to use when your program requires objects that contain similar number and kinds of variables and use similar functions.

Most Content Management Systems used on websites (e.g., WordPress) make use of classes and instances. One of the classes that WordPress has is wp_post. Instances of this class often contain a single blog or page post in a WordPress website.

Some of the attributes that the wp_post has are id, post_author, post_title, post_date, and post_content. The wp_post class is written inside the wp-includes/class-wp-post.php module. By the way, WordPress is written in PHP.

Writing Parent and Child Classes

If you are going to write a basic version of wp_post class in Python, it might look like this:

```
>>> class wp_post:
    post_id = ""
    post_author = ""
    post_title = ""
    post_content = ""
    def __init__(self):
        print("Instance of wp_post class created.")
    def displayAttributes(self):
        print("Title: " + self.post_title)
        print("Author: " + self.post_author)
        print("ID: " + self.post_id)
        print("Content: " + self.post_content)

>>> _
```

For the sake of the next examples, this example will supposedly be saved in the directory as class_wp_post.py.

To assign a value to an attribute, you can simply access it from the instance using the accessor operator (.) and assign a value to it. For example:

```
>>> from class_wp_post import wp_post
>>> post1 = wp_post()
Instance of wp_post class created.
>>> post1.post_id = 1
>>> post1.post_title = "This is a new website!"
>>> post1.post_author = "It's Me, Mario"
>>> post1.post_date = "January 1, 2010"
>>> post1.post_content = "Hello World!"
>>> post1.displayAttributes()
Title: This is a new website!
Author: It's Me, Mario
ID: 1
Content: Hello World!
>>> _
```

Default Attribute Value

You can set default values for the attribute by simply assigning them a value when they are declared outside methods. For example:

```
>>> class wp_post:
    post_id = "1"
    post_author = "None"
    post_title = "Untitled"
    post_content = "No Content"

>>> post1 = wp_post()
>>> post1.post_id
'1'
>>> _
```

Modifying Attribute Values

You can change the value of an attribute or attributes by accessing them from the instance using the accessor operator (.) and assigning them the value that you want. For example:

```
>>> class wp_post:
    post_id = "1"
    post_author = "None"
    post_title = "Untitled"
    post_content = "No Content"

>>> post1 = wp_post()
>>> post1.post_id = 10
>>> post1.post_id
10
>>> _
```

Inheritance

Inheritance is the ability of a class to inherit or copy another class' attributes and methods. When inheritance is involved in making classes, classes can be divided into two: parent and child.

Parent (also called super, base, and ancestor) classes are where child classes inherit or copies attributes and properties from. Child, also called sub, derived and descendant, classes copy attributes and methods from parent classes.

However, be aware that child classes do not *completely* copy all methods. To be precise, they do not copy constructors (__init__()) and destructors (__del__()).

Defining Attributes and Methods for the Child Class

Inheritance is useful if you work with multiple classes with common attributes and methods. For example:

```python
>>> class staff():
    name = ""
    gender = ""
    age = ""
    employee_id = ""
    def setDetails(self, name, gender, age, employee_id):
        self.name = name
        self.gender = gender
        self.age = age
        self.employee_id = employee_id

    def getDetails(self):
        print("Name: " + self.name)
        print("Gender: " + self.gender)
        print("Age: " + self.age)
        print("ID: " + self.employee_id)

>>> class supervisor(staff):
    team_members = []

>>> class cashier(staff):
    team_supervisor = ""

>>> class waiter(staff):
    team_supervisor = ""

>>> _
```

For convenience, this example is saved as a module with the file name **class_staff.py** and will be used in other examples that need it.

In this example, all instances created from the supervisor, cashier, and waiter classes will have all the attributes and methods of the staff class. For example:

```python
>>> import class_staff
```

```
>>> s1 = class-staff.supervisor()
>>> s1.getDetails()
Name:
Gender:
Age:
ID:
>>> s1.setDetails("John Doe", "Male", 25, 100001)
>>> s1.getDetails()
Name: John Doe
Gender: Male
Age: 25
ID: 100001
>>> _
```

As you can see, despite being an instance of the supervisor class, the instance was able to use the methods written for the staff class.

Using Pass

There are times that you do not have any attributes or methods to assign a child class. Unfortunately, Python's syntax does not allow an empty indented block or a statement with no indentation after a class and function declaration. For example:

```
>>> class parent():
...
  File "<stdin>", line 2
    ^
IndentationError: expected an indented block
>>> _
```

To avoid getting this error, you can use the pass keyword.

```
>>> class parent():
    pass

>>> class child(parent):
    pass

>>> _
```

Defining a purposeless variable would work, too. For example:

```
>>> class parent():
    uselessVariable = ""
```

```
>>> _
```
But this method is inefficient and confusing.

The init() Method For Child Class

It has been said that inheritance does not include constructors and destructors. This means that you should set the constructors and destructors method for each class that you make.

However, what if you want to use the __init__() method of your parent class for your child classes? It can be easily done by calling the __init__() method of the parent class. Here is a modified version of the previous example:

```
>>> class staff():
    name = ""
    gender = ""
    age = ""
    employee_id = ""
    def __init__(self, name, gender, age, employee_id):
        self.name = name
        self.gender = gender
        self.age = age
        self.employee_id = employee_id

    def getDetails(self):
        print(self.name)
        print(self.gender)
        print(self.age)
        print(self.employee_id)

class supervisor(staff):
    def __init__(self, name, gender, age, employee_id):
        super().__init__(name, gender, age, employee_id)
    team_members = []
class cashier(staff):
    def __init__(self, name, gender, age, employee_id):
        super().__init__(name, gender, age, employee_id)
    team_supervisor = ""
class waiter(staff):
    def __init__(self, name, gender, age, employee_id):
        super().__init__(name, gender, age, employee_id)
    team_supervisor = ""
```

```
>>> _
```

In here, each child class modified its own __init__() method. In the __init__() method, there is only one statement. The statement accesses and calls the parent class' __init__() method and passes the parameter values as arguments to the parent's __init__() method's parameters. It can be confusing at first since it might appear that you are just writing parameters instead of actually assigning arguments.

You might notice that there are three things missing in the statement. First, the parent class' object is missing. Second, the super() function that was placed. Third, the "self" argument was not passed as an argument.

The super() function acts as replacement and an implicit method to access the parent class. Also, using the super() built-in automatically passes the "self" argument to the __init__() method.

Aside from that, super is a cleaner and efficient way to handle child classes with multiple parent classes. Yes, a child class can have multiple parents just like parent classes can have multiple child classes.

Overriding methods from the parent class

There will be times when you want a certain child class' method to behave differently than the method written in the parent class.

Also, there will be times that you want to add a few more actions to the parent's method for a certain child class. To get through those scenarios efficiently and easily, you can override the parent's methods inside the child class. For example:

```
>>> class parent():
    def someFunction():
        print("This is the original function")

>>> class child1(parent):
    pass

>>> class child2(parent):
    def someFunction():
        print("This is an overridden function")

>>> x = child1()
>>> y = child2()
>>> x.someFunction()
This is the original function
>>> y.someFunction()
This is an overridden function
```

```
>>> _
```

In the example, there are three classes: parent(), child1(parent), and child2(parent). The parent class has a method called someFunction(). Since the child1() only passes, it will inherit the method someFunction(). On the other hand, child(2) has defined a method someFunction() similar to the parent's someFunction(), but with different statements.

When you call the sameFunction() method in an instance created from the child2() class, it will use the sameFunction() code written in child2() instead of the one written in parent() despite being a parent of the child2() class.

How about if you want to add some statements to the parent's method for one of the child classes? You can do it by defining the method on the child class. Then call the parent's method, and write the statements that you want to add.

Here is how you do it:

```
>>> class parent():
    def someFunction(self):
        print("This is the original function")

>>> class child1(parent):
    pass

>>> class child2(parent):
    def someFunction(self):
        super().someFunction()
        print("This is additional code")

>>> x = child1()
>>> y = child2()
>>> x.someFunction()
This is the original function
>>> y.someFunction()
This is the original function
This is additional code
>>> _
```

This is similar to how you override the __init__() method in the previous sections. By the way, always remember to add the "self" parameter to methods that you want to override when you use the super() function.

The super() function always send a reference to the object that calls the method. And if you use super() on a parent method without parameters, it would return an error. For example:

```
>>> class parent():
    def someFunction():
        print("Something.")

>>> class child1(parent):
    def someFunction():
        super().someFunction()
        print("Something Something")

>>> x = child1()
>>> x.someFunction()
Traceback (most recent call last):
  File "<stdin>", line 1, in <module>
TypeError: someFunction() takes 0 positional arguments but 1 was given
```

Importing Classes

To import classes, you can treat classes as if they are functions from a module. Of course, save the classes on a module first. By the way, some of the previous examples took advantage of importing classes if you have noticed.

For example:

```
>>> class staff():
    name = ""
    gender = ""
    age = ""
    employee_id = ""
    def setDetails(self, name, gender, age, employee_id):
        self.name = name
        self.gender = gender
        self.age = age
        self.employee_id = employee_id

    def getDetails(self):
        print("Name: " + self.name)
        print("Gender: " + self.gender)
        print("Age: " + self.age)
        print("ID: " + self.employee_id)

>>> class supervisor(staff):
    team_members = []
```

```
>>> class cashier(staff):
    team_supervisor = ""

>>> class waiter(staff):
...    team_supervisor = ""

>>>  _
```

Save this to class_staff.py. Then import it just like a module.

```
>>> import class_staff
>>> x = class_staff.cashier()
>>> x.getDetails()
Name:
Gender:
Age:
ID:
>>>  _
```

If you do not want to access the module name every time you use the class, you can always use the *from* and *import* combination. You can load the child class alone if you want. Python usually import the code for the parent if it is on the same module.

However, that is a practice that may form a habit, which is a bad one. There are times when the codes for the parent and child classes are saved in different modules. When you only import the child class in that situation, it might result in an error.

For example, say that the code for the staff() class is saved on module1.py and the supervisor(staff) class is saved on module2.py.

```
>>> from module2 import supervisor
Traceback (most recent call last):
  File "<stdin>", line 1, in <module>
  File "<C:\Python\module2.py", line 1, in <module>
    class supervisor(staff):
NameError: name 'staff' is not defined
>>>  _
```

To solve this, you must make sure that you import the parent classes first even if they are in the same module to prevent any error from popping up.

```
>>> from module1 import staff
>>> from module2 import supervisor
```

```
>>> x = supervisor()
>>> x.getDetails()
Name:
Gender:
Age:
ID:
>>> _
```

By the way, note that you should name modules as if you are creating an identifier in Python. This means that letters, numbers, and underscores are the only characters that you are allowed to use in the module's file name. Here is what will happen if you do not follow this:

```
>>> import class-staff
  File "<stdin>", line 1
    Import class-staff
                    ^
SyntaxError: invalid syntax
>>> _
```

Name Mangling

Name mangling is a naming technique in Python used to create "private" and "hidden" attributes. As you already know, variables used in functions become local variables. These local variables are inaccessible outside the scope of the function. However, variables that become attributes in classes are always accessible by using the accessor operator (.).

In some cases, you might want some of the attributes in your classes inaccessible outside but still accessible within the class. This is done through name mangling.

To mangle an attribute, all you need to do is to place two trailing underscores before a variable. For example:

```
>>> class someClass():
    variable1 = 0
    __variable2 = 0

>>> x = someClass()
>>> x.variable1
0
>>> x.__variable2
Traceback (most recent call last):
  File "<stdin>", line 1, in <module>
```

```
AttributeError: 'someClass' object has no attribute '__variable2'
>>> _
```

You may be wondering, where did __variable2 go? You see, when you mangle an attribute in Python, its identifier changes to this format: _<class name>__<attribute>. So, variable __variable2 will become _someClass__variable2.

```
>>> class someClass():
        variable1 = 0
        __variable2 = 0

>>> x = someClass()
>>> x.variable1
0
>>> x._someClass__variable2
0
>>> dir(x)
['__class__', '__delattr__', '__dict__', '__dir__', '__doc__', '__eq__', '__format__', '__ge__', '__getattribute__', '__gt__', '__hash__', '__init__', '__init_subclass__', '__le__', '__lt__', '__module__', '__ne__', '__new__', '__reduce__', '__reduce_ex__', '__repr__', '__setattr__', '__sizeof__', '__str__', '__subclasshook__', '__weakref__', '_someClass__variable2', 'variable1']
>>> _
```

What is self

You have already been exposed to the "self" argument in the past few sections. But, what is it exactly?

Self is a variable by convention that can be used as an argument to contain a reference to the object using it. By convention, it means that usage of the "self" variable is something that programmers formed as a habit and practice. Python does not force anyone to use the "self" identifier or variable in method definitions.

Nonetheless, we can double check if it does really contain an object by using this simple code.

```
>>> class sample():
        def check(self):
            return self

>>> x = sample()
>>> y = sample()
>>> x == x.check()
True
```

```
>>> x == y
False
>>> x == x
True
>>> id(x)
4319280
>>> id(x.check())
4319280
>>> _
```

In the above example, we have created the class sample(). The class contains a method named check() that contains the parameter and argument self. The method returns the value of check when called.

Then, the example created two instances of the sample() class: x and y. The example then checked if object x is equal to the "self" argument that the method check() will return. The comparison returns True.

To double check, objects x and y were compared, and it returns False. Then the ids of object x and the "self" argument were checked. Both had the same id.

The "self" variable is handy to use when referencing to the object that calls the method. After all, the method declaration cannot exactly include the possible names of the instances created using the class.

Since self is just an identifier, it is not a reserved keyword in Python. This means that you can actually use it as a variable, function, or class and assign something to it. It is encouraged to primarily use it for the purpose of readability, and it is highly discouraged to use it aside from the purpose of referencing the calling objects themselves.

And since it is only a convention, you can actually use other variables or parameters to catch the object reference. For example:

```
>>> class sample():
        def check(catcher):
            return catcher

>>> x = sample()
>>> x == x.check()
True
>>> id(x)
4319280
>>> id(x.check())
4319280
>>> _
```

Class and Static Methods

Methods in classes can be categorized into two: class and static methods. By default, all methods are automatically set as class methods.

The main difference between the two is that class methods automatically pass the calling object as an argument by reference while static methods do not. This is the reason it is required to have a self or any parameter that will receive the reference in class methods.

Without a parameter to catch the reference to the calling object, Python will return an error. For example:

```
>>> def sampleClass():
    def sampleFunction():
        print("Nothing")

>>> x = sampleClass()
>>> x.sampleFunction()
Traceback (most recent call last):
  File "<stdin>", line 1, in <module>
TypeError: sampleFunction() takes 0 positional arguments but 1 was given
>>> _
```

As you can see, Python detected that the class method call automatically sent a positional argument in form of the self object reference. And since the method sampleFunction() did not have any parameter to catch the argument, Python returned a Traceback TypeError.

Static methods, on the other hand, do not pass the any argument by default, so you can create methods that do not contain parameters.

In order to define class and static methods you need to use the decorator operator (@). For example:

```
>>> class classA():
    @classmethod
    def methodA():
        print("This is a Class Method.")

    @staticmethod
    def methodB():
        print("This is a Static Method.")

>>> class classB(classA):
    pass
```

```
>>> x = classB()
>>> x.methodB()
This is a Static Method.
>>> x.methodA()
Traceback (most recent call last):
  File "<stdin>", line 1, in <module>
TypeError: sampleFunction() takes 0 positional arguments but 1 was given
>>> _
```

The decorator operator (@) has other functionalities other than defining methods as static or class. However, it will not be discussed in this book.

Styling classes

- Always use "cls" as the first parameter for class methods.

- For instance methods, always use cls for the first argument.

- Method naming rules and conventions is similar to function and variable naming.

- Put a leading underscore in methods and variables you wish not to make public. They can still be seen during runtime, but the leading underscore will discourage other people to do something with methods and variables with it.

- Use name mangling if the methods and attributes you have in the super class will clash with the methods and attributes of a sub class.

- Of course, people have different views on name mangling. If it works for you, use it. You do not need to follow the style recommendations to the T.

- When it comes to naming classes it is advisable to use CapWords convention.

- You can use the naming convention for functions, methods, and variables if the class is primarily used to be called.

- The usage of CapWords on class names makes them completely distinguishable from built in names. The only objects that use the CapWords convention are built-in constants and exceptions.

Practice Exercise

Go to Amazon and look for three product categories. Create a super class with the name of AmazonProduct and a sub class for each of the product category.

Create three instances of each of the three product categories. After that, create a text-based system wherein you can buy and return the products.

Chapter Summary

Object oriented programming is certainly useful when you are developing a huge and scalable program. It organizes the data you input and output. In more advanced programs, classes can be helpful in other things such as creating templates for graphical user interfaces.

Just the understanding of what classes are can help you in programming in other languages. And it will also make it easy for you to understand programs and modules written by other people. After all, most of the advanced programs mostly use classes and subclasses.

Once again, a massive well done for your progress so far! Next up, you'll discover how to use files in your program. Let's get to it!

Chapter 6: Solution

```python
class AmazonProducts():
    pass

class WomensClothing(AmazonProducts):
    pass

class DollsAndAccessories(AmazonProducts):
    pass

class Books(AmazonProducts):
    pass

class Shorts(WomensClothing):
    pass

class Shirts(WomensClothing):
    pass

class Skirts(WomensClothing):
    pass

class Dolls(DollsAndAccessories):
    pass

class DollsClothes(DollsAndAccessories):
    pass

class DollsHouses(DollsAndAccessories):
    pass

class ChildrensBooks(Books):
    pass

class ComicBooks(Books):
    pass

class ChristianBooks(Books):
    pass
```

Did you know?

Computer programming is currently one of the fastest growing occupations. Majors related to computer programming are among the highest paying in colleges and universities. A programming language is basically a language that allows a human being to communicate with a computer. The lifestyle we live today with our tablets, and mobile phones wouldn't be possible without computer programming.

Chapter 7

Working With Files

Programs are made with input and output in mind. You input data to the program, the program process the input and it ultimately provides you with an output.

For example, a calculator will take in numbers and operations you want. It will then process the operation you wanted. And then it will display the result to you as its output.

There are multiple ways for a program to receive input and to produce output. One of those ways is to read and write data on files.

To start learning how to work with files, you need to learn the open() function.

The open() function has one *required* parameter and two *optional* parameters. The first and required parameter is the file name. The second parameter is access mode. And the third parameter is buffering or buffer size.

The file name parameter requires string data. The access mode requires string data, but there is a set of string values that you can use and is defaulted to "r". The buffer size parameter requires an integer and is defaulted to 0.

To practice using the open() function, create a file with the name sampleFile.txt inside your Python directory.

Try this sample code:

```
>>> file1 = open("sampleFile.txt")
>>> _
```

Note that the file function returns a file object. The statement in the example assigns the file object to variable file1.

The file object has multiple attributes, and three of them are:

- name: This contains the name of the file.

- mode: This contains the access mode you used to access the file.

- closed: This returns False if the file has been opened and True if the file is closed. When you use the open() function, the file is set to open.

Now, access those attributes.

```
>>> file1 = open("sampleFile.txt")
>>> file1.name
'sampleFile.txt'
>>> file1.mode
'r'
>>> file1.closed
```

False
>>> _

Whenever you are finished with a file, close them using the close() method.

```
>>> file1 = open("sampleFile.txt")
>>> file1.closed
False
>>> file1.close()
>>> file1.closed
True
>>> _
```

Remember that closing the file does not delete the variable or object. To reopen the file, just open and reassign the file object. For example:

```
>>> file1 = open("sampleFile.txt")
>>> file1.close()
>>> file1 = open(file1.name)
>>> file1.closed
False
>>> _
```

Reading from a File

Before proceeding, open the sampleFile.txt in your text editor. Type "Hello World" in it and save. Go back to Python.

To read the contents of the file, use the read() method. For example:

```
>>> file1 = open("sampleFile.txt")
>>> file1.read()
'Hello World'
>>> _
```

File Pointer

Whenever you access a file, Python sets the file pointer. The file pointer is like your word processor's cursor. Any operation on the file starts at where the file pointer is.

When you open a file and when it is set to the default access mode, which is "r" (read-only), the file pointer is set at the beginning of the file. To know the current position of the file pointer, you can use the tell() method. For example:

```
>>> file1 = open("sampleFile.txt")
```

```
>>> file1.tell()
0
>>> _
```

Most of the actions you perform on the file move the file pointer. For example:

```
>>> file1 = open("sampleFile.txt")
>>> file1.tell()
0
>>> file1.read()
'Hello World'
>>> file1.tell()
11
>>> file1.read()
''
>>> _
```

To move the file pointer to a position you desire, you can use the seek() function. For example:

```
>>> file1 = open("sampleFile.txt")
>>> file1.tell()
0
>>> file1.read()
'Hello World'
>>> file1.tell()
11
>>> file1.seek(0)
0
>>> file1.read()
'Hello World'
>>> file1.seek(1)
1
>>> file1.read()
'ello World'

>>> _
```

The seek() method has two parameters. The first is offset, which sets the pointer's position depending on the second parameter. Also, argument for this parameter is required.

The second parameter is optional. It is for whence, which dictates where the "seek" will start. It is set to 0 by default.

- If set to 0, Python will set the pointer's position to the offset argument.

- If set to 1, Python will set the pointer's position relative or in addition to the current position of the pointer.

- If set to 2, Python will set the pointer's position relative or in addition to the file's end.

Note that the last two options require the access mode to have binary access. If the access mode does not have binary access, the last two options will be useful to determine the current position of the pointer [seek(0, 1)] and the position at the end of the file [seek(0, 2)]. For example:

```
>>> file1 = open("sampleFile.txt")
>>> file1.tell()
0
>>> file1.seek(1)
1
>>> file1.seek(0, 1)
0
>>> file1.seek(0, 2)
11
>>> _
```

File Access Modes

To write to a file, you will need to know more about file access modes in Python. There are three types of file operations: reading, writing, and appending.

Reading allows you to access and copy any part of the file's content. Writing allows you to overwrite a file's contents and create a new one. Appending allows you to write on the file while keeping the other content intact.

There are two types of file access modes: string and binary. String access allows you to access a file's content as if you are opening a text file. Binary access allows you to access a file on its rawest form: binary.

In your sample file, accessing it using string access allows you to read the line "Hello World". Accessing the file using binary access will let you read "Hello World" in binary, which will be b'Hello World'. For example:

```
>>> x = open("sampleFile.txt", "rb")
>>> x.read()
b'Hello World'
>>> _
```

String access is useful for editing text files. Binary access is useful for anything else like pictures, compressed files, and executables. In this book, you will only be taught how to handle text files.

There are multiple values that you can enter in the file access mode parameter of the open() function. But you do not need to memorize the combination. You just need to know the letter combinations.

Each letter and symbol stands for an access mode and operation. For example:

- r = read only—file pointer placed at the beginning

- - r+ = read and write
- a = append—file pointer placed at the end
  - a+ = read and append
- w = overwrite/create—file pointer set to 0 since you create the file
  - w+ = read and overwrite/create
- b = binary

By default, file access mode is set to string. You need to add b to allow binary access. For example: "rb".

Writing to a File

When writing to a file, you must always remember that Python overwrites and not insert file. For example:

```
>>> x = open("sampleFile.txt", "r+")
>>> x.read()
'Hello World'
>>> x.tell(0)
0
>>> x.write("text")
4
>>> x.tell()
4
>>> x.read()
'o World'
>>> x.seek(0)
0
>>> x.read()
'texto World'
>>> _
```

You might have expected that the resulting text will be "textHello World". The write method of the file object replaces each character one by one starting from the current position of the pointer.

Practice Exercise

For practice, you need to perform the following tasks:

1. Create a new file named test.txt.

2. Write the entire practice exercise instructions on the file.

3. Close the file and reopen it.

4. Read the file and set the cursor back to 0.

5. Close the file and open it using append access mode.

6. Add a rewritten version of these instructions at the end of the file.

7. Create a new file and put similar content to it by copying the contents of the test.txt file.

Chapter Summary

Working with files in Python is easy to understand, but difficult to implement. As you already saw, there are only a few things that you need to remember. The hard part is when you are actually accessing the file.

Remember that the key things that you should master are the access modes and the management of the file pointer.

It is easy to get lost in a file that contains a thousand characters.

Aside from being versed with the file operations, you should also supplement your learning with the functions and methods of the str class in Python. Most of the time, you will be dealing with strings if you need to work on a file.

Do not worry about binary yet. That is a different beast altogether and you will only need to tame it when you are already adept at Python. As a beginner, expect that you will not deal yet with binary files that often contain media information.

Anyway, the next lesson is an elaboration on the "try" and "except" statements. You'll discover how to effectively manage and handle errors and exceptions.

Chapter 7: Solution

```
x = open("practice.txt", "w+")
x.write("1. Create a new file named test.txt.")
x.write("2. Write the entire practice exercise instructions on the file.")
x.write("3. Close the file and reopen it.")
x.write("4. Read the file and set the cursor back to 0.")
x.write("5. Create a new file and put similar content to it by copying the contents of the test.txt file.")
x.close()
x = open("practice.txt", "r")
x.read()
'1. Create a new file named test.txt.2. Write the entire practice exercise instructions on the file.3. Close the file and reopen it.4. Read the file and set the cursor back to 0.5. Create a new file and put similar content to it by copying the contents of the test.txt
 file.'
x.seek(0)
x.close
y = open("practice.txt", "w+")
x = open("practice.txt", "r")
text = x.read()
y.write(text)
y.close
x.close
```

Did you know?

Some programs are designed to steal your data or damage your computer. These programs are called malware. Viruses, worms, and trojans are all types of malware. You should be careful online, to avoid accidentally downloading malware!

Chapter 8

Exception Handling

What Is Exception Handling

Exception handling is error management. It has three purposes.

1. It allows you to debug your program.

2. It allows your program to continue running despite encountering an error or exception.

3. It allows you to create your customized errors that can help you debug, remove and control some of Python's nuances, and make your program function as you want it to.

Handling the Zero Division Error Exception

Exception handling can be an easy or difficult task depending on how you want your program to flow and your creativity. You might have scratched your head because of the word creativity. Programming is all about logic, right? No.

The core purpose of programming is to solve problems. A solution to a problem does not only require logic. It also requires creativity. Have you ever heard of the phrase, "Think outside of the box?"

Program breaking exceptions can be a pain and they are often called bugs. The solution to such problems is often elusive. And you need to find a workaround or risk rewriting your program from scratch.

For example, you have a calculator program with this snippet of code when you divide:

```
>>> def div(dividend, divisor):
        print(dividend / divisor)

>>> div(5, 0)
Traceback (most recent call last):
  File "<stdin>", line 1, in <module>
  File "<stdin>", line 2, in div
ZeroDivisionError: division by zero
>>> _
```

Of course, division by zero is an impossible operation. Because of that, Python stops the program since it does not know what you want to do when this is encountered. It does not know any valid answer or response.

That being said, the problem here is that the error stops your program entirely. To manage this exception, you have two options. First, you can make sure to prevent such operation from happening in your program. Second, you can let the operation and errors happen, but tell Python to continue your program.

Here is what the first solution looks like:

```
>>> def div(dividend, divisor):
    if (divisor != 0):
        print(dividend / divisor)
    else:
        print("Cannot Divide by Zero.")


>>> div(5, 0)
Cannot Divide by Zero.
>>> _
```

Here is what the second solution looks like:

```
>>> def div(dividend, divisor):
    try:
        print(dividend / divisor)
    except:
        print("Cannot Divide by Zero.")


>>> div(5, 0)
Cannot Divide by Zero.
>>> _
```

Remember the two core solutions to errors and exceptions. One, prevent the error from happening. Two, manage the aftermath of the error.

Using Try-Except Blocks

In the previous example, the try except blocks was used to *manage* the error. However, you or your user can still do something to screw your solution up. For example:

```
>>> def div(dividend, divisor):
    try:
        print(dividend / divisor)
    except:
        print("Cannot Divide by Zero.")


>>> div(5, "a")
Cannot Divide by Zero.
>>> _
```

The statement prepared for the "except" block is not enough to justify the error that was created by the input. Dividing a number by a string does not actually warrant a "Cannot Divide by Zero." message.

For this to work, you need to know more about how to use except block properly. First of all, you can specify the error that it will capture and respond to by indicating the exact exception. For example:

```
>>> def div(dividend, divisor):
    try:
        print(dividend / divisor)
    except ZeroDivisionError:
        print("Cannot Divide by Zero.")

>>> div(5, 0)
Cannot Divide by Zero.
>>> div(5, "a")
Traceback (most recent call last):
  File "<stdin>", line 1, <module>
  File "<stdin>", line 3, in div
TypeError: unsupported operand type(s) for /: 'int' and 'str'
>>> _
```

Now, the error that will be handled has been specified. When the program encounters the specified error, it will execute the statements written on the "except" block that captured it. If no except block is set to capture other errors, Python will then step in, stop the program, and give you an exception.

But why did that happen? When the example did not specify the error, it handled everything. That is correct. When the "except" block does not have any specified error to look out for, it will capture any error instead. For example:

```
>>> def div(dividend, divisor):
    try:
        print(dividend / divisor)
    except:
        print("An error happened.")

>>> div(5, 0)
An error happened.
>>> div(5, "a")
An error happened.
>>> _
```

That is a better way of using the "except" block if you do not know exactly the error that you might encounter.

Reading an Exception Error Trace Back

The most important part in error handling is to know how to read the trace back message. It is fairly easy to do. The trace back message is structured like this:

<Traceback Stack Header>
  <File Name>, <Line Number>, <Function/Module>
<Exception>: <Exception Description>

Here are things you need to remember:

- The trace back stack header informs you that an error occurred.

- The file name tells you the name of the file where the fault is located. Since the examples in the book are coded using the interpreter, it always indicated that the file name is "<stdin>" or standard input.

- The line number tells the exact line number in the file that caused the error. Since the examples are tested in the interpreter, it will always say line 1. However, if the error is found in a code block or module it will return the line number of the statement relative to the code block or module.

- The function/module part tells what function or module owns the statement. If the code block does not have an identifier or the statement is declared outside code blocks, it will default to <module>.

- The exception tells you what kind of error happened. Some of them are built-in classes (e.g., ZeroDivisionError, TypeError, and etcetera) while some are just errors (e.g., SyntaxError). You can use them on your except blocks.

- The exception description gives you more details with regards to how the error occurred. The description format may vary from error to error.

Using exceptions to prevent crashes

Anyway, to know the exceptions that you can use, all you need to do is to generate the error. For example, using the TypeError found in the previous example, you can capture that error too and provide the correct statements in response.

```python
>>> def div(dividend, divisor):
    try:
        print(dividend / divisor)
    except ZeroDivisionError:
        print("Cannot Divide by Zero.")
    except TypeError:
        print("Cannot Divide by Anything Other Than a Number.")
    except:
```

```
            print("An unknown error has been detected.")

>>> div(5, 0)
Cannot Divide by Zero.
>>> div(5, "a")
Cannot Divide by Anything Other Than a Number.
>>> div(undeclaredVariable / 20)
An unknown error has been detected.
>>> _
```

However, catching errors this way can still be problematic. It does allow you to prevent a crash or stop, but you have no idea about what exactly happened. To know the unknown error, you can use the *as* keyword to pass the Exception details to a variable. Convention wise, the variable detail is often used for this purpose.

For example:

```
>>> def div(dividend, divisor):
        try:
            print(dividend / divisor)
        except Exception as detail:
            print("An error has been detected.")
            print(detail)
            print("Continuing with the program.")

>>> div(5, 0)
An error has been detected.
division by zero
Continuing with the program.
>>> div(5, "a")
An error has been detected.
unsupported operand type(s) for /: 'int' and 'str'
Continuing with the program.
>>> _
```

The Else Block

There are times that an error happens in the middle of your code block. You can catch that error with try and except. However, you might not want to execute any statement in that code block if an error happens. For example:

```
>>> def div(dividend, divisor):
        try:
```

```
        quotient = dividend / divisor
    except Exception as detail:
        print("An error has been detected.")
        print(detail)
        print("Continuing with the program.")
    print(str(dividend) + " divided by " + str(divisor) + " is:")
    print(quotient)

>>> div(4, 2)
4 divided by 2 is:
2.0
>>> div(5, 0)
An error has been detected.
division by zero
Continuing with the program.
5 divided by 0 is:
Traceback (most recent call last):
  File "<stdin>", line 1, in <module>
  File "<stdin>", line 8, in div
    Print(quotient)
UnboundLocalError: local variable 'quotient' referenced before assignment
>>> _
```

As you can see, the next statements after the initial fault are dependent on it thus they are also affected. In this example, the variable quotient returned an error when used after the try and except block since its supposed value was not assigned because the expression assigned to it was impossible to evaluate.

In this case, you would want to drop the remaining statements that are dependent on the contents of the try clause. To do that, you must use the else block. For example:

```
>>> def div(dividend, divisor):
    try:
        quotient = dividend / divisor
    except Exception as detail:
        print("An error has been detected.")
        print(detail)
        print("Continuing with the program.")
    else:
        print(str(dividend) + " divided by " + str(divisor) + " is:")
        print(quotient)

>>> div(4, 2)
```

```
4 divided by 2 is:
2
>>> div(5, 0)
An error has been detected.
division by zero
Continuing with the program.
>>> _
```

The first attempt on using the function with proper arguments went well.

On the second attempt, the program did not execute the last two statements under the else block because it returned an error.

The else block always follows except blocks. The function of the else block is to let Python execute the statements under it when the try block did not return and let Python ignore them if an exception happens.

Failing Silently

Silent fails or failing silently is a programming term often used during error and exception handling.

In a user's perspective, silent failure is a state wherein a program fails at a certain point but never informs a user.

In a programmer's perspective, silent failure is a state wherein the parser, runtime development environment, or compiler fails to produce an error or exception and proceed with the program. This often leads to unintended results.

A programmer can also induce silent failures when he either ignores exceptions or bypasses them. Alternatively, he blatantly hides them and creates workarounds to make the program operate as expected even if an error happened. He might do that because of multiple reasons such as the error is not program breaking or the user does not need to know about the error.

Handling the File Not Found Exception Error

There will be times when you will encounter the FileNotFoundError. Handling such error depends on your intent or purpose with regards to opening the file. Here are common reasons you will encounter this error:

- You did not pass the directory and filename as a string.
- You misspelled the directory and filename.
- You did not specify the directory.

- You did not include the correct file extension.

- The file does not exist.

The first method to handle the FileNotFoundError exception is to make sure that all the common reasons do not cause it. Once you do, then you will need to choose the best way to handle the error, which is completely dependent on the reason you are opening a file in the first place.

Checking If File Exists

Again, there are always two ways to handle an exception: preventive and reactive. The preventive method is to check if the file exists in the first place.

To do that, you will need to use the os (os.py) module that comes with your Python installation. Then, you can use its path module's isfile() function. The path module's file name depends on the operating system (posixpath for UNIX, ntpath for Windows, macpath for old MacOS). For example:

```
>>> from os import path
>>> path.isfile("random.txt")
False
>>> path.isfile("sampleFile.txt")
True
>>>
```

Try and Except

You can also do it the hard way by using try, except, and else blocks.

```
>>> def openFile(filename):
    try:
        x = open(filename, "r")
    except FileNotFoundError:
        print("The file '" + filename + "' does not exist.")
    except FileNotFound:
        print("The file '" + filename + "' does exist.")

>>> openFile("random.txt")
The file 'random.txt' does not exist.
>>> openFile("sampleFile.txt")
The file 'sampleFile.txt' does exist.
>>>
```

Creating a New File

If the file does not exist, and your goal is to overwrite any existing file anyway, then it will be best for you to use the "w" or "w+" access mode. The access mode creates a new file for you if it does not exist. For example:

```
>>> x = open("new.txt", "w")
>>> x.tell()
0
>>> _
```

If you are going to read and write, use "w+" access mode instead.

Practice Exercise

Try to break your Python by discovering at least ten different exceptions.

After that, create a loop.

In the loop, create ten statements that will create each of the ten different exceptions that you find inside one try block.

Each time the loop loops, the next statement after the one that triggered an exception should trigger another and so on.

Provide a specific except block for each one of the errors.

Chapter Summary

Exception handling skills are a must learn for beginners. It teaches you how to predict, prevent, and manage exceptions. It allows you to test and debug your program and generate compromises with your skill, program, and system's limits.

That being said, you have made great strides to get this far and I commend you! However, you're now on the final stretch. In the next (and final) chapter, you'll discover how to test your code. See you there!

Chapter 8: Solution

```
a = 1
b = 0

while(True):
    try:
        c = a / b
        e = c + d
    except ZeroDivisionError:
        b = 1
        print("Zero Division Error")
    except NameError:
        d = "2"
        print("Name Error")
    except TypeError:
        print("Type Error")
        break
```

Did you know?

Spacecraft often run using old-fashioned computer systems because engineers are confident their programs do the job well and making a new one is risky and expensive. NASA's reusable spacecraft, the Space Shuttle, went into space using a computer designed in the 1970s. It had less code than most of today's mobile phones!

Chapter 9

Testing Your Code

When creating a program, you do not just write code. You have to test it.

At this point, your only methods of testing your code are to run the script, wait for errors (if any) and test it using the interpreter.

Be that as it may, there is another method to test your code. And that is by using the unit test module. Inside the module, there are multiple functions you can use to test your code.

By the way, you may ask - why the need for a "unittest" if you can test your code by running it or checking it one by one inside the interpreter?

First, using unit test is ideal for messy code. If other people cannot read your code, then unit test to see things that might go wrong. Unit test is much easier than manually testing one line of spaghetti code.

Second, unit test is much faster to do. It is easy to test using the interpreter and running the script, but if you have hundreds of statements, unit test is the best way to go.

Testing a function

It is advisable to perform the unit test when the code is nearly finished. The biggest problem with unit testing is that it can waste time when performed at the wrong time repeatedly. This is debatable, however.

Anyway, create a unit test in a module. You can do it in an interpreter, but it can be inconvenient since running the test will automatically close the window.

The first step in creating a unit test code is to import the unittest framework. Then you need to define a unit test subclass with TestCase from unittest. For example:

```
import unittest
class Test1(unittest.TestCase):
```

To perform the testing, you need to create methods for the cases that you want to test.

Note that most methods that you will inherit from the TestCase super class are assert methods (e.g., assertEqual(), assertNotEqual(), assertIs(), etcetera). These methods often have two parameters with assertTrue(), assertFalse(), assertIsNone(), and assertIsNotNone() having one parameter only.

These two parameters of most assert methods are tested according to the assert method used.

For example, assertEqual() checks if parameter a is equal to parameter b. If it is equal, it will return a passing mark. If it is not, it will return a failing mark. For example:

```
import unittest
class Test(unittest.TestCase):
    def test1(self):
        self.assertEqual(1, 1)

unittest.main()
```

To run the test, you must execute the main() callable of the unittest framework. Once executed, it will execute all the test that you created. After that, it will print information about the test on the console. This information includes error, score, and time consumed.

To have a little bit control in the test execution, add an input() function in the beginning of the script. For example:

```
import unittest

input("Press enter to start the test.")
class Test(unittest.TestCase):
    def test1(self):
        self.assertEqual(1, 1)

unittest.main()
```

If you run this test, it will display this information.

```
Press enter to start the test.
.
----------------------------------------------------------------
Ran 1 test in 0.000s

OK
```

The information tells the developer that it ran the single test method in the script and it took less than 0.0001 seconds to finish it. Since it immediately displayed the test result and OK line, that means it found no error.

The test1() method passed since 1 is equal to 1.

Here is an example that will result to an error:

```
import unittest

input("Press enter to start the test.")
```

```
class Test(unittest.TestCase):
    def test1(self):
        self.assertEqual(1, 0)

unittest.main()
```

Press enter to start the test.
F
==
FAIL: test1 (__main__.test)

Traceback (most recent call last):
  File "C:\P37\test.py", line 6, in test1
    self.assertEqual(1, 0)
AssertionError: 1 != 0

Ran 1 test in 0.000s

FAILED (failures=1)

The method to use when testing a function depends on the purpose of a function. But generally, all you need to do is to include one of the methods inside your TestCase's class. For example:

```
import unittest

input("Press enter to start the test.")
def onlyReturn1():
    return 1
def onlyReturn2():
    return "2"
class Test(unittest.TestCase):
    def test1(self):
        self.assertIsInstance(onlyReturn1(), int)
        self.assertIsInstance(onlyReturn2(), int)

unittest.main()
```

Press enter to start the test.
F
==
FAIL: test1 (__main__.test)

```
Traceback (most recent call last):
  File "C:\P37\test.py", line 11 in test1
    self.assertIsInstance(onlyReturn2(), 0)
AssertionError: '2' is not an instance of <class 'int'>


----------------------------------------------------------------

Ran 1 test in 0.000s

FAILED (failures=1)
```

By checking the context of the program, it is expected that the functions onlyReturn1() and onlyReturn2() should only return int class objects. To check that, the example use assertIsInstance() method.

Since onlyReturn2() returns a string value ('2'), the test failed. You may have noticed that there were more than one assert methods in the test method, but it only returned an error for one line and the result said it only ran 1 test.

One test method equates to one test. Also, when a test encounters failure, it stops processing the rest of the method since it basically received an exception.

Testing a Class

Testing a class is similar to testing a function. Remember that unittesting is used to make sure that functions, methods, and classes are passing off the correct and expected data.

Practice Exercise

For this chapter, your practice exercise is to create at least ten test methods and check the programs you made. Remember that the practice exercise chapter that told you to create the eight programs you listed? Yes. Those are the programs that you should use your unit tests on.

If you have not created those programs yet, you should try and do so now. You are more than ready to program with Python, and surely, you can make a decent version of the programs you wanted.

Chapter Summary

Unit testing is important in large scale and enterprise level program. It is something that is good to know. I encourage you to practice so that you'll eventually get to know the ins and outs of unit testing.

Check out Python's documentation about unit testing to discover other assertion tests. There are a lot, but they are easy to understand once you already performed a successful unit test.

Chapter 9: Solution

```python
import unittest

class Test(unittest.TestCase):
    def test1(self):
        self.assertEqual(1, 1)

    def test2(self):
        self.assertNotEqual(1, 0)

    def test3(self):
        self.assertTrue(True)

    def test4(self):
        self.assertTrue(False)

    def test5(self):
        self.assertIs(1, int())

    def test6(self):
        self.assertIsNot(1, str())

    def test7(self):
        self.assertIsNone(1)

    def test8(self):
        self.assertIsNotNone(0)

    def test9(self):
        self.assertIn(1, [2, 3, 4, 5])

    def test10(self):
        self.assertNotIn(1, [1, 2, 3, 4, 5])

unittest.main()
```

What Comes after This?

At this point, the most important thing for you to do is to practice programming in Python. If you have read this book in one to ten sittings, then you have already absorbed so much. You need to practice all the things you have learned to make sure you consolidate that knowledge (i.e. make it stick).

Remember that knowledge is useless without application. Learning how to program without actually programming will only waste the time you invested in this book. It is like learning how to ride a bike by reading books or articles about it - that will never be enough! You need to *ride* a bike to learn how to ride a bike.

Also, make sure to familiarize yourself with useful resources you can easily refer to when you need help. There are three obvious ones: Python's documentation, Stack Exchange, and this book.

During your programming journey, you will encounter seemingly impossible problems. Always get help if you encounter those problems. And during those times, never hesitate to reach out for help.

Finally, it's been an absolute pleasure taking you through this learning process and I wish you the very best of luck as you further explore the exciting world of programming!

The End

Thank you very much for taking the time to read this book. I tried my best to cover as much as I could to get beginner Python programmers off to a good start. If you found it useful please let me know by leaving a review on Amazon! Your support really does make a difference and I read all the reviews personally so can I understand what my readers particularly enjoyed and then feature more of that in future books.

I also pride myself on giving my readers the best information out there, being super responsive to them and providing the best customer service. If you feel I have fallen short of this standard in any way, please kindly email me at james.tudor@yahoo.com so I can get a chance to make it right to you. I wish you all the best with your programming journey!

Made in the USA
Columbia, SC
22 January 2021